The Official
Driver Theory Test
Trucks and Buses (Inc. Step 1 and 2 of Driver CPC)

Questions and Answers

Published by Prometric Ireland Limited under licence from the Road Safety Authority.

© 2019 Údarás Um Shábháilteacht Ar Bhóithre / Road Safety Authority

June 2019 Edition

ISBN 978-1-9160514-5-4

Prometric
La Touche House
Custom House Dock
IFSC
Dublin 1
DO1 R5P3
IRELAND

Foreword

As a learner driver, it is important that you have all the information you need to drive safely on our roads. Before you drive a Bus or Truck on public roads or in public places you must have a learner permit or a driving licence for the vehicle you want to drive. In most cases you must also pass a driver theory test to show that you understand what you must do to drive safely. The questions in the Truck and Bus driver theory tests, which are all in this book, are designed to test your knowledge and also to make you think about the different situations you will come across as a driver. If you wish to become a professional Truck or Bus Driver, you must also complete the mandatory Certificate in Professional Competence process (Driver CPC). This book contains questions from the Bus and Truck theory tests (Including Stage 1 of Driver CPC) as well as the case studies for Driver CPC - CPC Case Study theory test (Stage 2 of Driver CPC).

By studying the learning material and passing the Bus and/or Truck theory test you will have taken an important first step to becoming a safe driver. To be a professional driver you must also take the second step of passing the CPC Case study test. In order to be a safe & socially responsible driver, it is essential that you apply this knowledge and understanding whenever you are driving.

Learning to drive needs your time and patience, and the best way to learn is to take driving lessons from an approved driving instructor and get as much practice as you can

Finally, remember that driving should be enjoyable, and we wish you many years of safe driving.

Introduction and how to obtain a driving licence

Section 1: Trucks and Buses (Inc. Step 1 and 2 of Driver CPC)

Section 2: Case Studies

Introduction

To drive a motor vehicle on the public road in Ireland, you must hold a driving licence or a learner permit that covers the particular category of vehicle you plan to drive. For licensing purposes, there are fourteen categories of vehicle, identified by code letters – for example a Truck is Category C, a bus is Category D.

- To obtain a learner permit, you must pass a driver theory test – that is what this book is about.
- To obtain a full driving licence, you must first hold a learner permit, and develop your ability to drive the vehicle in a safe and socially responsible way, you must then pass a practical driving test.

With a learner permit, a number of restrictions apply, the most important of which is that you must be accompanied at all times by the holder of a full driving licence.

Who must take the driver theory test?

Before you can apply for your first learner permit in any driving licence category, you must have passed a driver theory test that relates to that category, and you must submit the driver theory test certificate to the licensing authority within two years of passing the test.

There are four different driver theory tests; which one you take depends on the category of vehicle you are planning to drive. This book covers all questions for the Truck and Bus driver theory tests, and different parts of the book are relevant to each test, as shown below.

If you wish to become a professional Truck or Bus Driver or drive a truck under the age of 21 years or bus under the age of 24 years then, you must also complete the mandatory Certificate in Professional Competence process (Driver CPC). This book contains case studies for the completion of the Driver CPC- CPC Case Study theory test. The table below also shows what parts of the book you should study to sit a CPC Case Study test.

Important: You must hold a full Category B Driving licence before you can book a driver theory test for a truck or bus theory test.

Category of vehicle you intend to drive		Parts of this book you need to study for driver theory test	Parts of this book you need to study to complete Driver CPC Case Study Test
C	Truck	Parts 1	Part 2
CE	Truck with trailer	Parts 1	Part 2
C1	Small truck	Parts 1	Part 2
C1E	Small truck and trailer	Parts 1	Part 2
D	Bus	Parts 1	Part 2
DE	Bus with trailer	Parts 1	Part 2
D1	Minibus	Parts 1	Part 2

Note that you do not have to pass the same theory test more than once. For example, if you pass the theory test for category C and obtain a learner permit for category C1, and you subsequently wish to obtain a learner permit for category CE, you are not required to take another driver theory test, provided you still have a valid learner permit or driving licence for category C.

In addition if you take and pass your Bus theory test now you can then choose to add the truck category at anytime in the following two years by sitting a shorter theory test of just 40 questions. These theory tests are known as either a Bus Module theory test or a Truck Module theory test

Preparing for the driver theory test

You should use this book and/or The Official Driver Theory Test Truck and Bus Questions and Answers CD-ROM as well as the Rules of the Road to prepare for the driver theory test. This book contains questions that you will be asked in your Truck and/or Bus driver theory tests, along with the correct answer and a brief explanation. Should you wish to become a professional driver of a truck or bus, this book also contains case studies for the CPC Case Study Theory Test that you will need.

If you spend sufficient time and effort preparing for your test, you should not find it difficult, and you should pass. More importantly, the knowledge you gain in preparing for the test will help to make you a better safe and socially responsible driver.

About the questions and answers in this book

In this book, you are presented with a question, the correct answer and an explanation (contained in the blue text box) as to why the answer is correct. Some questions may show a graphic which requires interpretation. For example:

What does this sign mean?
Crosswinds.

ABMW0099R

This sign gives advance warning that there may be crosswinds ahead. Crosswinds can affect the stability of your vehicle on the road.

In the test, you will be asked 100 questions and to pass you must answer at least 74 correctly. The questions will be taken from those set out in this book – you will not get a question that is not in the book.

In the test, each question you are asked is accompanied by four possible answers. Only one of these answers is correct, and you are required to identify it. The test is computerised and you will get a chance to practice before the test, so that you are familiar with the format.

Preparing for the CPC Case Study theory test

To prepare for your Truck or Bus CPC Case Study Theory Test you should study the following publications;

- This book-The Official Driver Theory Test Truck and Bus Questions and Answers plus CPC Case Studies or The Official Driver Theory Test CD-ROM Truck and Bus Questions and Answers plus CPC Case Studies
- The Rules of the Road
- Driving Goods Vehicles-The Official Driver Standards Agency (DSA) UK Guide

Or if you are doing the Bus Theory Test

- Driving Buses and Coaches-The Official Driver Standards Agency (DSA) UK Guide

In addition, the RSA have approved Driver CPC Training Centres which will help you in passing the Driver CPC Tests. A list of all RSA approved training centres is available on www.rsa.ie

The CPC Case Studies are short scenarios that describe various situations a bus or truck driver might face. There are 3 case studies with 15 questions in each case study (45 in total). To pass, you must correctly answer 28 of the 45 questions. You must answer correctly at least 5 questions on each case study.

Applying for a driver theory test

When you feel that you are well-enough prepared, apply to the Official Driver Theory Testing Service in one of the following ways:

Online:	www.theorytest.ie.
By telephone:	For an English language test call: 1890 606 106 For an Irish language test call: 1890 606 806
By post:	Complete an application form (obtainable from The National Driver Licensing Service (NDLS) or online from: www.theorytest.ie) and post it to: The Driver Theory Testing Service, PO Box 15, Dundalk, Co. Louth. When applying, please specify any special needs or language requirements that you have, so that appropriate arrangements may be made.

When booking a test, please have to hand credit/debit card details and your PSC Number.

Information on where and when theory tests may be taken can be obtained by contacting the Driver Theory Testing Service as above.

How to Obtain a Category C or D Driving Licence
Category C & D Licencing Process for Non-Professional Drivers

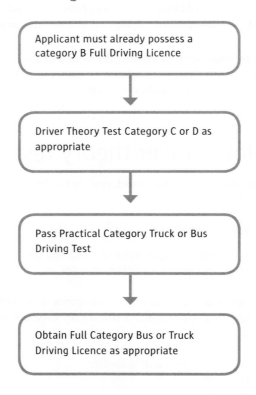

Applicant must already possess a category B Full Driving Licence

↓

Driver Theory Test Category C or D as appropriate

↓

Pass Practical Category Truck or Bus Driving Test

↓

Obtain Full Category Bus or Truck Driving Licence as appropriate

Minimum Age Requirements

- You must be a min. of 21 years of age to drive a Category C licence (truck) for **non-professional use.**
- You must be a min. of 24 years of age to drive a Category D (bus) for **non-professional use.**

However you may obtain a driving licence at the lower ages set out below:

- You must be a minimum of 18 years of age to apply for a first time Category C Driving licence with a CPC qualification to **drive professionally.**
- You must be a minimum of 21 years of age to apply for a first time Category D Driving licence with a CPC qualification to **drive professionally.**

How to Obtain a Category C or D Driving Licence
Category C & D Licencing Process for Professional Drivers (Min)

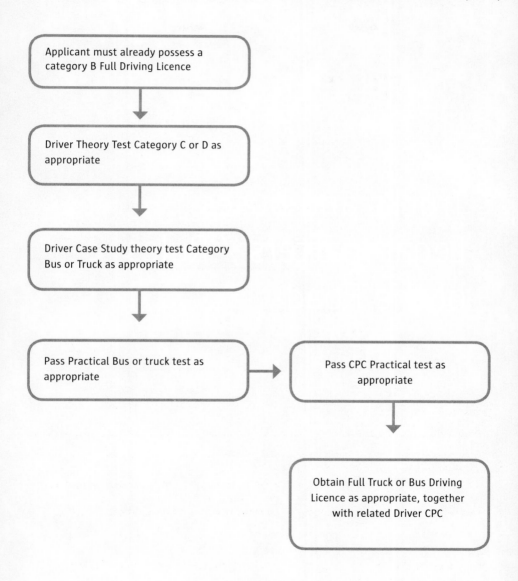

Applicant must already possess a category B Full Driving Licence

Driver Theory Test Category C or D as appropriate

Driver Case Study theory test Category Bus or Truck as appropriate

Pass Practical Bus or truck test as appropriate

Pass CPC Practical test as appropriate

Obtain Full Truck or Bus Driving Licence as appropriate, together with related Driver CPC

Section 1

Trucks and buses
Legal matters / Rules
of the Road

Driver Records / Driver Cards

Who is responsible for making sure that a driver's card is properly CD0181R
inserted into the digital tachograph unit?
The driver of the vehicle.

Driver smart cards were introduced to prevent driving hours offences. The regulations require the driver to insert their driver smart card into the digital tachograph unit when taking charge of a vehicle.

What records must be produced by a driver to an enforcement officer at a
roadside inspection? CD0184R
Any manual records used by the driver for the 28 calendar days immediately preceding that day.

Driving hours, rest periods and breaks are recorded by a tachograph, either digitally on the driver card or graphically on a tachograph chart. Drivers are legally required to carry records of activity for the preceding 28 days and to produce these records for inspection when requested by enforcement officers.

What driver records must be produced by a driver to an enforcement
officer at a roadside inspection? CD0185RU19
The driver's card.

Driving hours, rest periods and breaks are recorded by a tachograph, either digitally on the driver card or graphically on a tachograph chart. Drivers are legally required to carry records of activity for the preceding 28 days and to produce these records for inspection when requested by enforcement officers.

A driver is required to drive two or more vehicles fitted with digital
tachographs at different times during their working day. One of the
vehicles is used during a period which is exempt and 'out of scope' from
driver's hours and tachograph requirements. What should the driver do?
Use the tachograph's manual input facility to record 'other work'. CD0186R

Where a driver performs both 'in-scope' and 'out-of-scope' (exempt driving) in the same week, the out-of-scope driving can be recorded by manual entry on the digital tachograph unit.

A driver is working away from a vehicle and the driver's card is not inserted in the digital tachograph. What should the driver do? CD0189R
Manually enter times and activities in the tachograph.

Driver smart cards were introduced to prevent driving hours offences. If at the start of the working day a driver is engaged in non-driving duties away from the vehicle, they should manually enter a record of the other work activities into the digital tachograph when they take the vehicle in charge.

How long may a driver continue to drive without a driver card if their card has been lost or stolen? CD1300
15 days.

Driver smart cards were introduced to prevent driving hours offences. The regulations require the driver to insert their driver smart card into the digital tachograph unit when taking charge of a vehicle. If a card is lost or stolen the regulations require it be replaced promptly.

What should a driver do with a driver card that has malfunctioned?
Return it to the Road Safety Authority. CD1301

Driver smart cards record personalised data about the driver and their driving activity, and play a central role in preventing driving hours offences. Malfunctioning cards should be returned to the Road Safety Authority so they can be disposed securely and analysed if necessary.

How often must the data on a driver card be downloaded? CD1302
Every 21 days.

Driver smart cards were introduced to prevent driving hours offences. The regulations require that the data on the cards be downloaded every 21 days.

Who should a professional driver notify if his tachograph card is lost or stolen?

RSA01029

Gardaí and Road Safety Authority

For lost/stolen cards only: bring your application to a Gardaí station. The Gardaí must complete, sign and stamp the Gardaí Report on Section 1. If your digital tachograph card is lost, stolen, damaged, or malfunctioning, you should apply to the Road Safety Authority to have it replaced as soon as possible. If your digital tachograph card is damaged or malfunctioning, it must be returned to the Road Safety Authority with your application for a replacement.

Who is responsible for the long term storage of tachograph data after 21 days?

RSA01030

Operator

Operators/Companies must keep a copy for at least one year of both driver tachograph data as well as those from Vehicle Units (or mass memory) and therefore regularly download.

Who should you notify if your tachograph card is damaged?

RSA01031

Road Safety Authority

For damaged cards only: send your card to the RSA (with your application).

1

2

Driving Hours / Breaks Regulations

What is the maximum permitted number of hours that a driver can drive without taking a break?
CD0006R

4.5 hours.

You are required to take a rest period after 4.5 hours driving.

What is the maximum number of hours that a driver can drive in a given week?
CD0007R

56 hours.

EU regulations specify that a driver can drive no more than 56 hours in a given week.

What is the maximum permitted number of driving hours in a two-week period?
CD0008

90 hours.

EU regulations specify that a driver can drive no more than 90 hours in a two-week period.

What is the minimum break time that should be taken for each break during or following a driving period?
CD0009R

15 minutes.

EU regulations specify that a driver must take a break of at least 15 minutes during or following a driving period.

What is the minimum break time which must be taken following a 4.5 hour driving period?
CD0010R

45 minutes.

EU regulations specify that a driver must take a break of at least 45 minutes after driving for 4.5 hours.

What is the maximum number of hours a driver may drive in week two, if 56 hours were worked in week one?
CD0011R

34 hours.

EU regulations specify that a driver can drive no more than 90 hours in a two-week period.

On how many days of the working week may a driver drive for more than 9 hours?
CD0012R

2 Days.

EU regulations on driving hours were introduced to reduce the incidence of driver fatigue, which is a known risk factor in road collisions. These regulations specify that a driver must not drive for more than 56 hours a week, with a maximum of 10 hours a day for two days, 9 hours a day for four days and at least one full rest day.

On how many days of the working week may a driver drive?
CD0013R

6 Days.

EU regulations on driving hours were introduced to reduce the incidence of driver fatigue, which is a known risk factor in road collisions. These regulations specify that a driver must not drive on more than six days in any week and must not exceed 56 driving hours in the week.

On three days of the week what can the minimum daily rest period be reduced to?
CD0014R

9 hours.

EU regulations on driving hours were introduced to reduce the incidence of driver fatigue, which is a known risk factor in road collisions. These regulations specify that a driver must take an 11-hour rest period within each 24-hour period. This may be reduced to 9 hours on a maximum of three days in a two-week period.

What is the normal minimum weekly rest period?
CD0015R

45 consecutive hours.

EU regulations on driving hours were introduced to reduce the incidence of driver fatigue, which is a known risk factor in road collisions. These regulations specify that a driver must normally take two rest periods, each of 45 consecutive hours, in a two-week period.

On a rest day, may a driver carry out other 'paid duties' apart from driving?
CD0016R

No. It is a rest day.

EU regulations on driving hours were introduced to reduce the incidence of driver fatigue, which is a known risk factor in road collisions. These regulations specify that a driver is not permitted to do any paid work on a rest day, driving or otherwise.

Under what circumstances can a driver's rest period be taken in a parked vehicle?
CD0031R

If the vehicle is fitted with a bunk.

Drivers are required to take a daily rest period of at least 11 hours. This can be broken down into one uninterrupted period of 3 hours and a second uninterrupted period of at least 9 hours. Drivers may take their rest periods in a parked vehicle only if the vehicle is fitted with a bunk.

According to EU driver's hours regulations, a break is required for the driver after driving
CPC1098

four and a half hours.

This is EU law as set by Council Rules (EEC) 3820/85 and 561/2006.

Under EU drivers hours regulations, what is the minimum number of consecutive hours of daily rest a driver must take?
CPC1100

11 reduced to 9.

This is EU law as set by Council Rules (EEC) 3820/85 and 561/2006. It is also Irish law and helps make our roads safer.

After four and a half hours of driving, how long a break must a driver take?
CPC1290

45 minutes.

Under EU rules, after driving no more than 4.5 hours you must take a break of at least 45 minutes unless you take a rest period.

What is the maximum time a driver can drive between weekly rest periods?
CPC1291

56 hours.

There is a maximum weekly driving limit of 56 hours and you must take a weekly rest period after no more than six daily driving periods. You may drive up to 56 hours between weekly rest periods. Rules set under EU 561/2006.

Under EU driving hours regulations, what is the maximum hours that may be driven in a given week?
CPC1294

56 hours.

Under EU rules (EU 561/2006), the maximum weekly driving limit is 56 hours.

Under EU driving hours regulations, the shortest break that a driver can take in a driving period is
CPC1295

15 minutes.

Under EU and Irish law, your first break from driving must be at least 15 minutes.

Under EU drivers' hours regulations, a driver must take a break after how many hours driving?
CPC1385

4.5 hours.

EU rules state that all drivers must take an uninterrupted break of 45 minutes after four and a half hours of driving. You could face fines and lose your licence if you don't comply.

Under EU drivers' hours regulations, after driving for four and a half hours, a driver must take an uninterrupted break of
CPC1386

45 minutes.

You must take a break of at least 45 minutes after 4.5 hours of driving. It also helps make our roads safer.

Under EU drivers' hours regulations, a 'day' means a period of
CPC1387

24 hours.

Under EU rules, a day is defined as any 24-hour period beginning when you start driving after your last daily or weekly rest period.

1
2

Hand Signals / Garda Signals

What does this hand signal mean? ABMW0140RU19

The cyclist intends to move out or turn right.

This hand signal tells other road users that the cyclist intends to either move out or make a right hand turn. Drivers should be aware that cyclists could move out into the path of their vehicle without looking.

What does this hand signal mean? ABMW0141RU19

The cyclist intends to slow down or stop.

This hand signal informs other road users that cyclist intends to slow down or stop. This may indicate that the cyclist is aware of some hazard ahead, so drive with extra care.

What does this hand signal mean? ABMW0144RU19

The cyclist intends to turn right.

This hand signal tells other road users that the cyclist intends to either move out or make a right hand turn. Drivers should be aware that cyclists could cross the path of their vehicle.

What does this hand signal mean? ABMW0151RU19

The driver intends to proceed straight ahead.

This hand signal informs other road users or a garda directing traffic that the driver intends to proceed straight ahead.

Industry Regulation

When driving a truck with hazardous goods or substances, who is responsible for ensuring that a Hazchem sign is displayed? C0078U19
The driver.

When driving a truck carrying hazardous goods, drivers must ensure that the correct symbol or mark is clearly displayed on the vehicle. In the event of a collision, the information provided by the sign provides vital information for the emergency services.

Which of the following operators requires a Road Haulage Operator's Licence? C1314U19
An operator that is transporting a customer's goods for hire.

A Road Haulage Operator's Licence is required to carry goods for hire or reward in a vehicle or combination of vehicles that has a maximum authorised mass greater than 3.5 tonnes.

A driver who transports dangerous goods must have which of the following? C1325
An ADR Driver Training Certificate.

A driver who transports dangerous goods must be certified on the specific technical requirements that have to be met during transport of dangerous goods. This certification is the ADR Driver Training Certificate.

Who enforces the licensing provisions of the Road Transport Acts? CD1349
The Road Safety Authority and An Garda Síochána.

The Road Safety Authority is responsible for enforcing the licencing provisions of the Road Transport Acts.

Road Haulage and Road Passenger Transport Operator's Licenses are issued and maintained by CD1350
The Department of Transport.

The Department of Transport is the regulator for both passenger and road haulage operations.

Which of the following organisations is responsible for enforcing EU and national transport legislation on the licensing of road haulage and passenger operators? CD1351
The Road Safety Authority.

The Road Safety Authority is the regulator for both passenger and road haulage operations.

Licensing

When may a trailer be towed on a public road without a rear number plate? ABMW0211RU19

Never, a number plate must always be displayed.

The law requires all motorised vehicles to display a rear number plate that is clean and legible.

What category of licence must a driver hold in order to drive a vehicle with a Maximum Authorised Mass (M.A.M) of 7,500kgs with seating for no more than 8 passengers? C0001AA

Category C1, C1E, C or CE.

To drive a rigid vehicle with a design gross vehicle weight of between 3,500kg and 7,500kg, you must hold a category C1 licence. Above 7,500kg DGVW, you need a category C licence.

What is the Maximum Authorised Mass (M.A.M) of a vehicle that the holder of a category C1 licence may drive? C0002AA

7,500kgs.

To drive a rigid vehicle with a design gross vehicle weight of between 3,500kg and 7,500kg, you must hold a category C1 licence. Above 7,500kg DGVW, you need a category C licence.

Is the holder of a category C1 licence entitled to tow a trailer?

Yes, up to 750kgs Maximum Authorised Mass (M.A.M). C0007RA

If you hold a full category C1 licence, you may tow a trailer with a design gross vehicle weight of 750kg or less. However, if you hold a category C1 learner permit, you may not tow a trailer.

Is the holder of a category C learner permit entitled to tow a trailer when driving a category C vehicle? C0008RA

No, the holder of a category C learner permit must not tow a trailer.

If you hold a learner permit for category B, C1, C, D1 or D, you may not tow a trailer. A full licence holder in one of these categories may tow a trailer with a design gross vehicle weight of 750kg or less.

Is the holder of a category C licence entitled to tow a trailer when driving a category C vehicle?

C0009RA

Yes, provided the trailer does not exceed 750kgs Maximum Authorised Mass (M.A.M).

If you hold a full category C licence, you may tow a trailer with a design gross vehicle weight of 750kg or less. However, if you hold a category C learner permit, you may not tow a trailer.

What is the maximum number of passengers that can be carried by the holder of a Category C or C1 licence?

C0010R

8 passengers.

If you hold a category C or C1 licence, you are permitted to drive vehicles with seating for up to 8 passengers plus the driver.

What does the term Maximum Authorised Mass (MAM) refer to?

C0012AU19

MAM refers to the term used by manufacturers for the weight of the vehicle together with the maximum load it is designed to carry.

Maximum Authorised Mass is the term used by manufacturers for the weight of the vehicle together with the maximum load it is designed to carry including passengers, fuel, cargo and attachments. The MAM is usually shown on a metal plate attached to the vehicle by the manufacturer.

What does this information sign indicate about the load when displayed on a truck or trailer?

C0013RA

Bio Hazard

This sign indicates the type of material carried and the level of hazard associated with it.

Which of the following vehicle types can the holder of a Category C1 driving licence drive?

C1315U19

A vehicle with a Maximum Authorised Mass (MAM) greater than 3,500 kgs but less than 7,500 kg.

A category C1 licence holder may drive a vehicle with a maximum authorised mass not exceeding 7,500 kg and with a seating capacity for up to 8 passengers.

Which of the following vehicle combinations can the holder of a Category C driving licence drive?

C1316U19

Any vehicle in category C towing a trailer not exceeding 750kgs.

The holder of a Category C licence may drive any category C vehicle whilst towing a trailer not exceeding 750 kgs.

Which of the following conditions must an applicant for a truck learner permit satisfy?

C1318U19

Be normally resident in Ireland.

An applicant for a truck learner permit must be at least 18 years of age, hold a category B Driving Licence and be normally resident in Ireland.

To apply for a Category C learner permit an individual must already hold a full driving licence in which of the following categories?

C1319U19

Category B.

To apply for a Category C learner permit an applicant must already be the holder of a full Category B driving licence.

To apply for a Category C1 learner permit an individual must already hold a full driving licence in which of the following categories?

C1320U19

Category B.

To apply for a Category C1 learner permit an applicant must already be the holder of a full Category B driving licence.

How frequently must a commercial vehicle be submitted for a Commercial Vehicle Roadworthiness Test (CVRT)?

CD0002U19

Annually.

All commercial vehicles – that is, goods vehicles, buses carrying more than 8 passengers, and ambulances – must, in general, be tested for roadworthiness (commercial vehicle roadworthiness test or CVRT) when they are one year old and annually after that.

What learner permit drivers in categories C, C1, D and D1 are required to be accompanied by the holder of a full licence?

CD0003R

All.

If you hold a learner permit for category C, C1, D or D1, you must be accompanied and supervised at all times while driving by someone who holds a current full driving licence for the same category of vehicle.

For learner permit holders driving a large vehicle, which is the MOST accurate statement about L plates?

CPC1119

They must be displayed in the front and rear of the vehicle.

Which of the following is true regarding periodic training requirements for Driver CPC? All drivers must take part in a minimum of

CPC1122U19

35 hours of training every five years.

A driver who has completed all of their periodic training is entitled to a Driver CPC card for a period of

CPC1123U19

5 years.

Drivers who have completed 7 hours periodic training per year over a 5 year cycle are entitled to receive a driver CPC card. As per EU directive 2003/59/EC.

Is the holder of a category D or D1 learner permit allowed to carry passengers for payment or reward while driving a bus?

D0003RU19

No.

The holder of a learner permit driving a car, van, bus or coach must not carry any passengers for payment of any kind.

Must the holder of a category D learner permit who holds a category D1 full licence display L plates on a bus or coach while taking driving lessons?

D0005RU19

Yes, at all times.

The holder of a learner permit (in every category except A1, A and M) must always display proper L-plates on the front and rear of the vehicle they are driving.

Must the holder of a category D learner permit who already holds a category D1 full licence be accompanied by the holder of a category D licence when driving a bus or coach?
D0006R

Yes, at all times.

A learner permit holder in category D must always be accompanied and supervised by the holder of a full licence in that category.

Is a driver who holds a full category D licence restricted to automatic transmission (code 78) permitted to drive a conventional manual bus or coach on that licence?
D0007R

No.

If you pass your driving test in a vehicle equipped with automatic transmission, a code 78 is noted in the restrictions column of your full licence. This restricts you to driving only vehicles with automatic transmission. If you subsequently wish to drive a manual vehicle in that category, you must obtain a new learner permit and comply with the regulations pertaining to learner permits, including L-plates and accompanying driver.

Who is required to hold a road passenger transport operator's licence?
A person or firm with a business involved in transporting persons by road for reward.
D0009R

In order to operate a business involved in the transport of persons for reward by road, the operator must hold a road passenger transport operator's licence. For the full period of validity of the licence, the operator must employ a transport manager who holds a certificate of professional competence in road passenger transport.

What is the maximum number of passenger seats in a vehicle that can be driven by the holder of a category D1 licence?
D0024RU19

16

If a driver holds a D1 driving licence, they are only allowed to drive a bus or coach with a maximum of 16 passenger seats.

Which of the following operators requires a Road Passenger Transport Operator's Licence?
D1306

An operator that is carrying 9 or more passengers for hire in a vehicle constructed to do so.

A Road Passenger Transport Operator's Licence is required to carry passengers by road for hire or reward in vehicles constructed and equipped to carrying nine or more passengers.

1

2

A Category D1 licence permits the holder to drive a vehicle which can carry a maximum of how many passengers, excluding the driver? D1316U19
16 passengers.

A Category D1 licence holder may drive a vehicle with seating for up to a maximum of 16 passengers, apart from the driver.

A Category (D1E) licence is required to drive which of the following vehicles? D1318U19
A vehicle that carries more than 8 passengers but not more than 16 excluding the driver, towing a trailer, where the combined Maximum Authorised Mass (MAM) is 12,000kg or less.

A Category D1E licence holder may drive a vehicle that carries more than 8 passengers but less than 16 passengers combined with a trailer if the maximum authorised mass of the trailer is greater than 750kg but less than 12,000kg

---

To apply for a bus learner permit an individual must satisfy which of the following conditions? D1320U19
Normally resident in Ireland.

To apply for a bus learner permit you must be at least 21 years of age and normally resident in Ireland.

To apply for a Category D learner permit an individual must already hold a licence in which of the following categories? D1321
B.

To apply for a Category D learner permit you must already hold a Category B licence.

To apply for a Category D1 learner permit an individual must already hold a licence in which of the following categories? D1322
B.

To apply for a Category D1 learner permit you must already hold a Category B licence.

To apply for a Category (DE) learner permit an individual must already hold a licence in which of the following categories?

D1323

D.

To apply for a Category DE learner permit you must already hold a Category D licence.

To apply for a Category (D1E) learner permit an individual must already hold a licence in which of the following categories?

D1324

D1.

To apply for a Category D1E learner permit you must already hold a Category D1 licence.

What is the minimum age at which a driver who holds a valid Driver CPC card can drive a 53-seater bus or coach?

RSA01002U19

21 years.

To avoid breaching the law it is essential to know and comply with all the licencing requirements. Whilst the general minimum age for driving a large bus or coach is 24 yrs. a driver may obtain a driving licence for Category D at the age of 21 if he/she also holds a Drivers Certificate of Professional Competence (CPC).

What is the minimum age at which a driver can drive a 14-seat bus?

21 years

RSA01003

To avoid breaching the law it is essential to know and comply with all the licensing requirements. The minimum age for driving a mini-bus is 21 years of age.

What is the minimum amount of periodic refresher training that the holder of a bus Driver CPC card must do, each year, to maintain their qualification?

RSA01005U19

Seven hours.

Once a bus driver obtains his/ her Driver CPC card they must then complete periodic refresher training to maintain it. In Ireland, periodic refresher training consists of a course of 35 hours broken down into 5 annual modules each lasting a minimum of 7 hours.

After what period is a bus on the road required to display a valid Commercial Vehicle Roadworthiness Test (CVRT) disc?

RSA01006U19

After 1 year.

All commercial vehicles must be tested when they are over one year old and annually after that. Commercial Vehicle Testing is one component of the preventative measures we need to have safer vehicles on our roads. The Commercial Vehicle Roadworthiness Test (CVRT) is a roadworthiness test for all commercial vehicles over one year old. The CVRT confirms that a vehicle satisfies basic safety standards on the day the test is carried out. It tests what is accessible and visible.

What rule applies to towing a trailer for a Category D1 learner permit holder?

RSA01007U19

The holder may not tow a trailer.

Category D1 drivers may not tow a trailer without holding a full licence in the category.

What is the legal requirement for any organised bus trip carrying children?

RSA01008U19

The bus must have appropriate and fit for purpose safety belts or restraint systems.

Important Regulations concerning children and safety belts on buses come into effect on the 31 October 2011. The Road Traffic (Restraint Systems in Organised Transport of Children) Regulations (Statutory Instrument No. 367 of 2011) make it a legal requirement that all buses involved in the organised transport of children must be fitted with appropriate and fit for purpose safety belts or restraint systems.

Which of the following is a condition of the 12 day rule for international coach journey?

The driver is on a single trip journey.

RSA01009U19

Professional drivers can only work for 12 consecutive days if they follow the rules before during and after their international coach tour trip.

Which of the following is a minimum rest period option that an international coach tour driver must take before using the 12 day rule?

RSA01010U19

Take a rest period of 45 hours immediately before the journey.

Professional coach drivers can only work for 12 consecutive days if they follow the rules before during and after their international coach tour trip.

Which of the following is a requirement of the 12 day rule for international coach tour driving after 1st January, 2014?

RSA01011

If the driving time is between 10pm and 6am, you must have more than one driver, or you can't drive more than 3 hours without a break.

Future requirements After 1st January, 2014, there will be 2 additional requirements for coach drivers taking 12 day trips (1)You must have a digital tachograph fitted to your vehicle (2)If your driving time is between 22:00 and 06:00, you must have more than one driver, or you can't drive more than 3 hours without a break.

Who is responsible for ensuring a valid Road Passenger Operators Licence Disc is affixed to the vehicle?

RSA01016

Vehicle Driver.

It is responsibility of a driver and operator, to put proper arrangements in place to make sure that, where relevant, each vehicle complies with the requirements to display the Road Passenger Operators Licence Disc.

What operator is exempt from carrying a Road Haulage Operators Licence?

RSA01017U19

An operator that owns a category C type truck and uses it to transport their own goods.

You need a Road Haulage Operators Licence if you are carrying goods for hire or reward in a vehicle or combination of vehicles the maximum authorised weight of which is in excess of 3.5 (metric) tonnes.

1

2

Offences / Penalties

How many penalty points collected in 36 months will result in a driving ban?
CPC1106A

12 Points.

This is part of the penalty point system under Irish law. You will be banned from driving if you collect 12 points in a 36 month period.

If a fixed charge notice is received, the fine must be paid within how many days to avoid additional penalty?
CPC1107A

28 Days.

This is the fixed charge system under Irish law. This gives you 28 days to pay the fixed charge. Failure to pay will increase the charge by 50% (if you pay within the next 28 days).

A fixed charge notice contains all of the following information EXCEPT
when to appear in court.
CPC1108

This is Irish law as set by Road Traffic Act 1961 - 2005 (Fixed Charge Offences) Rules 2006. Usually there would be no court appearance necessary providing the fixed charge is paid in time.

If 12 or more penalty points are built up in a 36 month period, how many months is the driver banned from driving?
CPC1109

6 months.

This is Irish law as set by Road Traffic Rules 2006. Note - If you are banned from driving you must submit your driving licence to the National Driver Licence Service within 14 days.

When a driver is disqualified from driving, within how many days must the licence be handed in to the Court for endorsement?
CPC1110AU19

14 Days.

A driver has to hand in their driving licence within 14 days - this is Irish law regarding driving bans.

Who is responsible for ensuring a vehicle is NOT transporting illegal immigrants?

CPC1188A

The driver.

You may face penalties if you bring illegal immigrants into the country in your vehicle, whether you know they are there or not.

After parking at a border crossing, who is responsible for checking that the vehicle has not been tampered with?

CPC1199A

The Driver

You should carry out all security and checks even more carefully when travelling abroad, especially if your vehicle has been unattended at any time when parked at a border crossing.

On an international journey, when should a driver check his/her vehicle?

At appropriate times throughout the journey.

CPC1202AU19

1

2

Carry out a security check before you drive your vehicle. Search your vehicle at the end of a route and before starting your return journey, to ensure that nothing has been concealed or left behind.

When travelling abroad, what should drivers do if they find a suspicious item within or around the vehicle?

CPC1209AA

Arrange for the appropriate authorities to deal with the item.

If you find unattended luggage, you should contact the company and arrange for it to be removed as soon as possible.

Which of the following may assist a driver to avoid penalties for carrying illegal immigrants?

CPC1215A

Making use of vehicle checks provided by port operators.

It is best practice to operate an effective system to protect your vehicle against carrying illegal immigrants. An effective system is made up of three parts – vehicle security, vehicle checking and documentation. This includes vehicle checks provided by Ports.

What are the three parts of an effective system to protect the driver against carrying illegal immigrants?

CPC1220

Vehicle security, vehicle checking, and documentation.

It is best practice to operate an effective system to protect your vehicle against carrying illegal immigrants. An effective system is made up of three parts – vehicle security, vehicle checking and documentation.

Which of these is one of the most common causes of criminal damage to vehicles?

CPC1425

Missile throwing.

The most common forms of criminal damage are missile throwing, slashed seats, graffiti and broken windows.

Which area of a vehicle must be checked for unauthorised access?

On the axles.

CPC1437U19

As well as checking the other areas, you must check the underside of the vehicle as illegal immigrants sometimes hide above the vehicle axle.

What is the number of penalty points on payment of a fine for a licensed bus driver travelling at 100Km/h on a national road?

RSA01004

Three Penalty points

The number of penalty points recorded under the fixed penalty points scheme for driving a bus at 100Km/h on a national road where the limit is 80km/h is set at three. This may increase to five penalty points following a court appearance.

Parking

Where is a driver allowed to park?
ABMW0189RU19

Where the driver is not blocking other road users their view of traffic signals or the road ahead.

It is an offence to park at the side of a road that has a single or double continuous white line along its centre. Parking on such a road could create an obstruction and may cause inconvenience or danger to other road users.

What distance before a zebra crossing is parking prohibited?
ABMW0190RU19

15 metres.

It is an offence to park 15 metres before or 5 metres after a pedestrian crossing. Parking in this manner may restrict the zone of vision of drivers approaching the crossing and endanger pedestrians.

Within what distance of a road junction is parking prohibited?
ABMW0191RU19

5 metres, unless parking spaces are clearly marked.

It is an offence to park within 5 metres of a road junction unless parking spaces are clearly marked. Parking in that area may restrict the zone of vision of drivers approaching the junction and may cause an obstruction to large vehicles wishing to turn.

Is a driver permitted to park at an entrance to a property?
ABMW0193RU19

Yes, with the property owner's consent.

You may park across the entrance to a property only with the owners consent. Parking across an entrance may cause inconvenience and danger to persons entering or leaving the property.

When is parking permitted on a footpath?
ABMW0194RU19

It is never permitted to park on a footpath.

It is an offence to park on a footpath. Where a vehicle is parked on a footpath, pedestrians may have to step onto the road to go around the vehicle and so place themselves in danger.

When is double parking permitted?

ABMW0195RU19

It is never permitted.

Double parking is never permitted. Parking is never permitted where it might interfere in any way with the normal flow of traffic or obstruct or endanger other road users.

When is parking permitted at a taxi rank?

ABMW0196RU19

Parking at a taxi rank is prohibited unless driving a taxi.

Stopping or parking within an area marked as a taxi rank is prohibited as this may obstruct taxis entering or leaving the rank.

When is parking permitted at a sharp bend?

ABMW0197RU19

Parking is never permitted at a sharp bend.

Parking is never permitted where it might interfere in any way with the normal flow of traffic or obstruct or endanger other road users – for example, by forcing other drivers into the path of oncoming traffic.

When is parking permitted on the brow of a hill?

ABMW0198RU19

Parking is never permitted on the brow of a hill.

Parking on the brow of a hill or on a humpbacked bridge is prohibited. Parking in such a place may restrict the zone of vision of drivers approaching the hill and force them into the path of oncoming traffic.

Regulatory Signs and Motorway Signs

ABMW0033RU19

What do these signs together mean?
Pedestrianised street ahead - traffic not allowed except during times shown.

When posted together these signs tells you that there is a Pedestrianised street ahead and that traffic is not allowed to enter except during the times stated on the information plate.

ABMW0034U19

What does this sign mean?
Maximum permitted weight is 3 tonnes.

This sign tells you that that you must not enter this area if your vehicle is over 3 tonnes or 3,000 kg

ABMW0037A

What does this sign mean?
Maximum permitted height of vehicle is the figure indicated.

This sign tells you that you must not enter this area if your vehicle exceeds the indicated height.

ABMW0039U19

What does this sign mean?
No overtaking.

This sign tells you that overtaking is prohibited. These signs are usually found in places where overtaking may be dangerous, such as in areas with reduced visibility.

ABMW0040RU19

What does this sign mean?
Only buses, cyclists and taxis are allowed to use the lane ahead during the hours indicated.

This sign tells you there is a with-flow near side bus lane ahead on the left – that is, one where the buses move in the same direction as the traffic to their right. The information plate tells the times when the bus lane is in operation. Only buses, taxis and cyclists may use the bus lane during those hours.

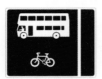

ABMW0041RU19

What does this sign mean?
With-flow bus and cycle lane ahead on left.

This sign tells you there is a with-flow near side bus lane ahead to the left. Only buses, taxis and cyclists may use the bus lane during the stated operational hours.

ABMW0042RU19

What does this sign mean?
With-flow bus and cycle lane on left.

This sign indicates a near side with-flow bus lane on the left. Only buses, taxis and cyclists may use the bus lane during the stated operational hours.

ABMW0043RU19

What does this sign mean?
Bus and cycle lane ahead on right.

This sign tells you that there is an off side bus lane ahead on the right. Only buses, taxis and cyclists may use the bus lane during the stated operational hours.

What does this sign mean?

With-flow bus lane on the right.

ABMW0044RAU19

This sign indicates a with-flow off-side bus lane on the right. Only buses, taxis and cyclists may use the bus lane during the stated operational hours.

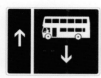

What does this sign mean?

Contra-flow bus lane on the right.

ABMW0045RU19

This sign tells you that you must drive on the left and not use the contra-flow bus lane day or night. A contraflow bus lane is one where the buses are going in the opposite direction.

What does this sign mean?

Contra-flow bus lane.

ABMW0046U19

This sign tells you that you must drive on the left and not use the contra-flow bus lane day or night. A contra-flow bus lane is one where the buses are going in the opposite direction.

What does this sign mean?

Tram lane on right.

ABMW0050RAU19

This sign tells you there is an off-side tram lane on the right. Drivers should also be aware that there might be pedestrians in the area.

1

2

What does this sign mean?
ABMW0109RU19

Entry to motorway.

This is a motorway information sign informing road users they are now entering the motorway and must obey motorway rules. This sign usually appears beside a motorway ahead sign.

What does this sign mean?
ABMW0110U19

Motorway ends 500 metres ahead.

This is a motorway information sign that tells you that the motorway will end in 500 metres ahead. Motorway rules will no longer apply, for example a lower speed limit may be applicable.

What does this sign mean?
ABMW0111RU19

End of motorway.

This sign indicates the end of the motorway. You are leaving the motorway and its rules will no longer apply.

At roadworks, what does this sign mean?
ABMW0132RU19

Proceed with caution.

This traffic control sign tells you that you may proceed with caution through road works.

At roadworks, what does this sign mean?
ABMW0133RU19

Stop before or at the sign.

This traffic control sign at roadworks means you must stop.

Speed Limits

Unless otherwise indicated, what is the maximum permissible speed of a car towing a trailer on national roads?
ABMW0187U19

80 Km/h.

When towing a trailer on a national road, it is illegal to exceed 80 Km/h – exceeding this speed will make the vehicle unstable.

Unless otherwise indicated, what is the maximum permissible speed of a car towing a trailer on a motorway?
ABMW0188AU19

80 Km/h.

When towing a trailer on a motorway it is illegal to exceed 80 Km/h – excessive speed may make such a vehicle unstable.

When do temporary speed limits apply at roadworks?
ABMW0221RU19

For the duration of the roadworks.

Temporary speed limits at road works apply for the duration of the works. When road works are completed, normal speed limits apply.

What is the maximum permitted speed of a truck?
C1300

90 km/h.

A truck is subject to a maximum speed limit of 90 km/h. This applies to motorway driving only, unless a lower speed limit is in place. Trucks are subject to a general speed limit of 80 km/h.

What is the maximum permitted speed of a truck on a motorway?
C1301

90 km/h.

A truck is subject to a speed limit of 90 km/h on a motorway, unless a lower speed limit is in place.

What is the maximum permitted speed of a truck on a national primary road?
C1302

80 Km/h.

A truck is subject to a general speed limit of 80 km/h, unless a lower or higher speed limit is in place.

What is the maximum permitted speed of a truck on a dual carriageway?
80 Km/h.
C1303

A truck is subject to a general speed limit of 80 km/h, unless a lower or higher speed limit is in place.

What is the maximum permitted speed on a motorway for a goods vehicle with a Maximum Authorised Mass (MAM) of more than 3,500kg?
90 Km/h.
C1304AU19

Goods Vehicles with a Maximum Authorised Mass (MAM) above 3,500 kg are not permitted to travel at a speed greater than 90km/h on motorways. Note : A general speed limit of 80 km/h applies on all other roads, unless a lower speed limit is in place.

What is the maximum permitted speed for a vehicle with a Maximum Authorised Mass (MAM) of 3,000kg?
C1305U19

120 Km/h.

Vehicles with a Maximum Authorised Mass(MAM) below 3,500 kg are subject to the speed limits which apply to cars and smaller vehicles, which is 120 km/h, unless a lower speed limit is in place.

What is the maximum permitted speed of a truck in an urban slow zone area?
C1306U19

30 km/h.

Trucks, like all vehicles, are subject to a speed limit of 30 kilometres per hour in urban slow zone areas

What is the maximum permitted speed of a truck on a regional or local road?

C1307U19

80 Km/h.

A truck is subject to a general maximum speed limit of 80 km/h on regional or local roads unless a lower speed limit is indicated.

What is the maximum permitted speed on a motorway of a single-decker bus or minibus (having passenger accommodation for more than 8 persons) and which is not designed to carry standing passengers?

100km/h.

D0060R

A single- or double-decker bus or coach that is not designed to carry standing passengers is subject to a general speed limit of 100km/h on motorways, unless a lower speed limit is in place.

What is the maximum permitted speed on a dual carriageway of a single-decker bus or minibus (having passenger accommodation for more than 8 persons) and which is not designed to carry standing passengers?

100km/h.

D0061R

A single- or double-decker bus or coach that is not designed to carry standing passengers is subject to a general speed limit of 100km/h on a dual carriageway, unless a lower speed limit is in place.

What is the maximum permitted speed on a national primary road of a single-decker bus or minibus (having passenger accommodation for more than 8 persons) and which is not designed to carry standing passenger?

80km/h.

D0062R

A single-decker bus or minibus that is not designed to carry standing passengers is subject to a general speed limit of 80km/h on national roads, and 100km/h on motorways and or dual carriageways, unless a lower speed limit is in place.

What is the maximum permitted speed on a motorway of a double-decker bus or minibus (having passenger accommodation for more than 8 persons) and which is not designed to carry standing passengers?

100km/h.

D0063R

A single- or double-decker bus or coach that is not designed to carry standing passengers is subject to a general speed limit of 100km/h on dual carriageways, unless a lower speed limit is in place.

What is the maximum permitted speed on a dual carriageway of a double-decker bus or minibus (having passenger accommodation for more than 8 persons) and which is not designed to carry standing passengers?
D0064R
100km/h.

A single- or double-decker bus or coach that is not designed to carry standing passengers is subject to a general speed limit of 100km/h on dual carriageways, unless a lower speed limit is in place.

What is the maximum permitted speed on a national primary road of a double-decker bus or minibus (having passenger accommodation for more than 8 persons) and which is not designed to carry standing passenger?
D0065R
80km/h.

A single-decker bus or minibus that is not designed to carry standing passengers is subject to a general speed limit of 80km/h on national roads, and 100km/h on motorways and dual carriageways, unless a lower speed limit is in place.

What is the maximum permitted speed on a motorway of a single-decker bus or minibus (having passenger accommodation for more than 8 persons) and which is designed to carry standing passengers?
D0066R
65km/h.

A single-decker bus or minibus that is designed to carry standing passengers is subject to a general speed limit of 65km/h on motorways, unless a lower speed limit is in place.

What is the maximum permitted speed on a dual carriageway of a single-decker bus or minibus (having passenger accommodation for more than 8 persons) which is designed to carry standing passengers?
65km/h.
D0067R

A single-decker bus or minibus that is designed to carry standing passengers is subject to a general speed limit of 65km/h on dual carriageways, unless a lower speed limit is in place.

What is the maximum permitted speed on a national primary road of a single-decker bus or minibus having passenger accommodation for more than 8 persons and which is designed to carry standing passengers?
65km/h.   D0068R

A single-decker bus or minibus that is designed to carry standing passengers is subject to a general speed limit of 65km/h on national and primary roads, unless a lower speed limit is in place.

What is the maximum permitted speed limit on a motorway of a double-decker bus or minibus (having passenger accommodation for more than 8 persons) and which is designed to carry standing passengers?
65km/h.   D0069R

A double-decker bus or minibus that is designed to carry standing passengers is subject to a general speed limit of 65km/h on motorways, unless a lower speed limit is in place.

1
2

What is the maximum permitted speed on a dual carriageway of a double-decker bus or minibus (having passenger accommodation for more than 8 persons) and which is designed to carry standing passengers?
65km/h.   D0070R

A double-decker bus or minibus that is designed to carry standing passengers is subject to a general speed limit of 65km/h on motorways, unless a lower speed limit is in place.

What is the maximum permitted speed on a national primary road of a double-decker bus or minibus (having passenger accommodation for more than 8 persons) and which is designed to carry standing passengers?
65km/h.   D0071R

A double-decker bus or minibus that is designed to carry standing passengers is subject to a general speed limit of 65km/h on motorways, unless a lower speed limit is in place.

Tachograph

What does this tachograph symbol mean?
Driving time.

CD0017RU19

Tachographs (recording devices) are required to be fitted to trucks over 3.5 tonnes and to buses with more than 9 seats. They record the drivers driving activity, rest periods, vehicle speed, distance travelled and other information. The driver should select the symbol that represents the activity they are engaged in – rest, driving or other work. The records must be retained for inspection by Enforcement Officers.

What does this tachograph symbol mean?
Other work.

CD0018RU19

Tachographs (recording devices) are required to be fitted to trucks over 3.5 tonnes and to buses with more than 9 seats. They record the drivers driving activity, rest periods, vehicle speed, distance travelled and other information. The driver should select the symbol that represents the activity they are engaged in – rest, driving or other work. The records must be retained for inspection by Enforcement Officers.

What does this tachograph symbol mean?
Other work - that is, work other than actual driving.

CD0019R

Tachographs (recording devices) are required to be fitted to trucks over 3.5 tonnes and to buses with more than 9 seats. They record the driver's driving activity, rest periods, vehicle speed, distance travelled and other information. The driver should select the symbol that represents the activity they are engaged in – rest, driving or other work. The records must be retained for inspection by Enforcement Officers.

What does this tachograph symbol mean?
Rest or break period.

CD0020RU19

Tachographs (recording devices) are required to be fitted to trucks over 3.5 tonnes and to buses with more than 9 seats. They record the drivers driving activity, rest periods, vehicle speed, distance travelled and other information. The driver should select the symbol that represents the activity they are engaged in – rest, driving or other work. The records must be retained for inspection by Enforcement Officers.

Who is responsible for ensuring that a tachograph record is properly completed and inserted into the tachograph?
CD0022RU19
The driver.

EU regulations require the driver to keep daily records. The driver is responsible for ensuring that the tachograph chart is properly completed and inserted into the tachograph.

What information is recorded on a tachograph record?
CD0023RU19
Driving time, vehicle speed and distance.

The tachograph chart records a drivers driving hours, vehicle speed, and distance covered. It is used to check that the driver takes at least the legal minimum amount of rest during the working day.

What information is recorded on a tachograph record?
CD0024RU19
Breaks and rest periods.

The tachograph chart records a drivers driving hours, vehicle speed, and distance covered. It is used to check that the driver takes at least the legal minimum amount of rest during the working day.

1

2

Which tachograph records must be retained by the driver?
CD0025R
Records for the current day and the 28 calendar days immediately preceding that day

The tachograph chart records a driver's driving hours, vehicle speed, and distance covered. It is used to check that the driver takes at least the legal minimum amount of rest during the working day. The regulations require the driver to keep records for the current and the previous 28 days, and to produce them on demand.

When must a new tachograph record be placed in a tachograph?
CD0026RU19
At the start of each working day.

EU regulations require the driver to keep daily records. The driver is responsible for ensuring that the tachograph chart is properly completed and inserted into the tachograph at the start of each working day.

What time and day denote the beginning of a week for tachograph purposes?

CD0027R

00.00 hours on Monday.

The tachograph chart records a driver's driving hours, vehicle speed, and distance covered. It is used to check that the driver takes at least the legal minimum amount of rest and does not exceed the legal maximum driving hours in a day, week or fortnight. For tachograph purposes, the week starts at 00.00 hours on Monday and finishes at 24.00 hours on Sunday.

If two drivers are intending to use the same vehicle in a given day what should the first driver do?

CD0029RU19

Remove their tachograph record when they leave the vehicle and insert it again when they recommence driving the vehicle.

EU regulations require that if a vehicle is being used by more than one driver in a given day, each driver should use their own tachograph chart for that day.

If, in a given day, two drivers intend to use the same vehicle fitted with a digital tachograph, what should the first driver do?

CD0180R

Remove their driver's card from the digital tachograph unit of the vehicle when they leave it.

EU regulations specify that if a vehicle is being driven by more than one driver in a given day, each driver must use their own driver's card in slot one of the digital tachograph unit while they are operating the vehicle and remove it when leaving the vehicle.

A driver did not use a tachograph chart on a new journey. Which of the following is the MOST severe penalty risk?

CPC1112U19

Imprisonment and/or heavy fine.

This is EU law as set by Council Regulation (EEC) 3821/85 and SI No. 89 European Communities (Road Transport) (Recording Equipment) Regulation 2006. These regulations are clear in setting out that offenders may be imprisoned and/or fined for infringements of these regulations.

A driver has driven a vehicle on a journey and has not used a tachograph. What is the MOST severe penalty risk?

CPC115B

Loss of licence and heavy fines.

This is EU law as set by Council Regulation (EEC) 3821/85 and SI No. 89 European Communities (Road Transport) (Recording Equipment) Regulation 2006.

A device that records hours of driving, breaks and rest periods is a

CPC1288

tachograph.

A tachograph is a measuring instrument that records hours of driving, breaks and rest periods as well as the distance you travel and speed you travelled at.

Traffic Controls

What is the purpose of traffic calming measures?
ABMW0210RU19

To slow down traffic in the vicinity.

The purpose of traffic calming measures is to slow down fast-moving traffic to a speed more suitable for the area they are entering. These measures are usually found in rural areas on the entry points to towns or villages.

Who can use a signed cycle track accompanied by a continuous white line on the left-hand side?
ABMW0213R

Cyclists and users of motorised wheelchairs.

A cycle track is for the use of cyclists and motorised wheelchairs only. No other vehicles may cross into or over a mandatory cycle track unless this is necessary in order to leave or enter a side road or a property adjacent to the cycle track.

What traffic may use a cycle lane accompanied by a continuous white line?
ABMW0214RU19

Cyclists and motorised wheelchairs.

A cycle track is for the use of cyclists and motorised wheelchairs. No other vehicles may cross into or over a mandatory cycle track unless this is necessary in order to leave a side road or a property adjacent to the cycle track.

Apart from cyclists and motorised wheelchairs, what other road users may use an unoccupied cycle lane accompanied by a broken white line?
ABMW0215RU19

All drivers may make temporary use.

Drivers may make tempoary use of a cycle track with a broken white line on the right hand side if it is not occupied.

When must drivers stop at an automated railway level crossing with barriers and red flashing lights?
ABMW0216RU19

Stop safely when the amber light shows, or when red lights start to flash.

You must stop safely when the amber light shows. Flashing red lights have the same meaning as a steady red traffic light - stop safely when they show.

At a railway level crossing with unattended gates, what should a car driver do?

ABMW0217RU19

Open both gates before proceeding to cross.

At a level crossing with unattended gates a driver must stop, look for trains and listen for the sound of a horn or approaching trains. If it is safe, open both gates, complete the crossing and then close both gates.

What lights indicate a zebra crossing?

ABMW0218R

Flashing amber beacons.

A zebra crossing is indicated by amber flashing beacons on poles and black and white stripes on the road. You must stop for pedestrians on the crossing and for those about to cross.

What does a continuous white line along the centre of the road mean?

ABMW0256RU19

No U-turn allowed.

You must never do a U-turn on any stretch of road with a continuous white line along its centre. The restricted vision at such places would make doing a U-turn very unsafe.

What does a continuous white line in the centre of the road mean?

ABMW0259RU19

Vehicles may not cross or straddle the line.

You must not cross or straddle a continuous white line in the centre of the road unless you wish to enter land or premises and it is safe to do so.

Traffic Controls » Parking

When wanting to stop temporarily in a congested area where should the driver park?
ABMW0331RU19
Park in a safe, legal and convenient place.

You should park only where it is safe, legal and convenient to do so. Your parked vehicle must not cause a danger or an obstruction to other road users. The use of hazard warning lights does not excuse unsafe or illegal parking.

What is a clearway?
ABMW0501RU19
An area where stopping and parking is not permitted during certain times.

A clearway is an area of road that must be kept clear for moving traffic during certain times of the day (usually busy periods). The times when stopping or parking is prohibited are shown on an information plate under the sign.

Traffic Controls » Regulatory

What does this sign mean?
ABMW0038U19
Parking of vehicles exceeding the weight shown is not allowed.

This sign tells you that you must not park in this area if your vehicle is over the weight limit indicated.

Traffic Controls » Traffic Lights

What does this traffic light mean?
ABMW0175U19

Traffic turning left may proceed if the way is clear.

A green arrow (filter light) means that traffic may proceed in the direction of the arrow if it is safe to do so.

When traffic lights are green, when should a driver not proceed?
ABMW0179RU19

When it would be unsafe to do so.

Although a green traffic light means proceed with caution, you should not enter a junction if the way is not clear or if by doing so you would cause an obstruction to other road users.

What does a flashing amber arrow pointing left at a traffic light mean?
ABMW0180RU19

A driver may turn left but yield to traffic on the other road.

A flashing left amber arrow at a junction means you may proceed left but must give way to pedestrians and traffic already coming through the junction on the other road.

What do flashing amber arrows indicate at a junction?
ABMW0219RU19

When safe, drivers should proceed in the direction indicated.

When you meet a flashing amber arrow at a junction, you should proceed in the direction indicated provided it is safe to do so.

What do temporary traffic lights at road works mean?
ABMW0220R

A driver must comply with the lights at all times.

You must comply with any temporary traffic lights used to control vehicle movements at or near road works. It is an offence not to obey these lights.

Traffic Signs » Regulatory

What does this sign mean?

ABMW1A

No entry to goods vehicles with five axles or more.

This sign tells you that heavy goods vehicles with five or more axles are not permitted to enter this road.

What does this sign mean?

ABMW2

Tram lane on left.

This sign tells you there is a tram lane on the left. Be aware that there might be pedestrians in the area and crossing the road.

Traffic Signs » Warning Signs

What does this sign mean?
Low bridge up ahead.

ABMW0078U19

This sign gives advance warning that you are approaching a low bridge, with restricted headroom as shown on the sign.

What does this sign mean?
Overhead electric cables.

ABMW0079

This sign gives advance warning of electric cables overhead. Drivers with a high load should be particularly careful.

What does this sign mean?
Crosswinds ahead.

ABMW0099RU19

This sign gives advance warning that there may be crosswinds ahead. Crosswinds can affect the stability of your vehicle on the road. Be prepared to slow down if necessary.

Traffic Signs » Warning Signs / Road Signs

What does this sign mean?

ABMW0052RU19

Y-Junction where main road bears to the left.

This sign gives advance warning of a Y-junction with a minor road ahead. The wider arm of the Y indicates the course of the main road.

What does this sign mean?

ABMW0054RU19

Crossroads ahead with roads of equal importance.

This sign gives advance warning of a crossroad junction ahead where the roads are of equal importance. At this type of junction you should yield to traffic approaching from the right and traffic already turning.

What does this sign mean?

ABMW0056RU19/57RU19

Y-junction ahead with roads of equal importance.

This sign gives advance warning of a Y-junction ahead with roads of equal importance. Approach such a junction with caution and be prepared to react to any changes in the traffic situation.

What does this sign mean?

ABMW0058RU19

Crossroads with major road ahead.

This sign gives advance warning of a crossroads junction with a major road ahead. Be prepared to stop.

What does this sign mean?

ABMW0059RU19

T-junction ahead with a road of major importance.

This sign gives advance warning of a T-junction ahead with a major road. Be prepared to yield or stop as necessary.

What does this sign mean?
ABMW0060RU19

Crossroads with dual carriageway ahead.

This sign gives advance warning of a crossroads junction at a dual carriageway ahead. Drivers need to be observant, taking extra care for traffic coming from each direction. Yield and/or stop as appropriate.

What does this sign mean?
ABMW0061RU19

T-junction with dual carriageway ahead.

This sign gives advance warning of a T-junction at a dual carriageway ahead. Drivers need to be observant, taking extra care for traffic coming from each direction. Yield and/or stop as appropriate.

What does this sign mean?
ABMW0062RU19

Traffic merging from the left.

This sign gives advance warning of traffic merging from the left. You should expect vehicles to join from the left. You may need to slow down, allowing them to merge safely.

What does this sign mean?
ABMW0063RU19

Traffic merging/diverging ahead.

This sign gives advance warning of roads both merging (entering onto the main road) and diverging (exiting the main road). Drivers should be prepared for traffic changing speed and direction as vehicles enter or exit at the junctions on the left ahead.

What does this sign mean?
ABMW0064RU19

Roundabout ahead.

This sign gives advance warning of a roundabout ahead. You must be prepared to yield to vehicles already on the roundabout or coming from the right.

1
2

What does this sign mean?
Mini-roundabout ahead.

ABMW0065RU19

This sign gives advance warning of a mini-roundabout ahead. You must be prepared to yield to vehicles already on the roundabout or coming from the right.

What does this sign mean?
Dangerous corner ahead.

ABMW0066U19

This sign gives advance warning of a dangerous corner to the left. You may need to slow down and react to any changes in the traffic situation ahead.

What does this sign mean?
Dangerous bend ahead.

ABMW0067U19

This sign gives advance warning of a dangerous bend to the left. You may need to slow down and react to any changes in the traffic situation ahead.

What does this sign mean?
Series of dangerous corners ahead.

ABMW0068U19

This sign gives advance warning of a series of dangerous corners ahead. You should slow down and react to any changes in the traffic situation.

What does this sign mean?
Series of dangerous bends ahead.

ABMW0069RU19

This sign gives advance warning of a series of dangerous bends ahead. You should slow down and react to any changes in the traffic situation.

What does this sign mean?
Sharp change of direction to the right.

ABMW0070RU19

This sign gives advance warning of a sharp change of direction to the right. You should slow down as you approach the hazard.

What does this sign mean?
ABMW0071RU19

Road narrows on the left.

This sign gives advance warning that the road narrows on the left ahead. You should show caution and prepare to adjust your road position.

What does this sign mean?
ABMW0072U19

Road narrows on both sides.

This sign gives advance warning that the road is narrowing on both sides ahead. You should show caution and prepare to slow down.

What does this sign mean?
ABMW0073RU19

Road divides ahead.

This sign gives advance warning that the road divides ahead. You should prepare to move to the left.

What does this sign mean?
ABMW0075U19

Two-way traffic ahead.

This sign gives advance warning of two-way traffic ahead, with oncoming traffic in the opposite lane.

What does this sign mean?
ABMW0076U19

Steep descent ahead.

This sign gives advance warning of a steep descent/downward slope ahead. You should react accordingly by adjusting speed and selecting the appropriate gear.

What does this sign mean?
ABMW0077U19

Steep ascent ahead.

This sign gives advance warning of a steep ascent/upward hill ahead. You should react by selecting the appropriate gear.

What does this sign mean?

ABMW0082U19

Level crossing ahead protected by lights and barriers.

This sign gives advance warning of a railway level crossing ahead protected by lights and barriers. The crossing may also have an audible warning alarm. You should be prepared to stop.

What does this sign mean?

ABMW0084RU19

Automatic level crossing ahead.

This sign gives advance warning of an automatic level crossing ahead. Drivers should approach with caution and be prepared to slow down or stop as necessary.

What does this sign mean?

ABMW0086RU19

Sharp depression or dip ahead.

This sign gives advance warning of a dip or depression in the road ahead which may be hidden and could obscure your view of oncoming traffic. You should reduce your speed accordingly and be aware that overtaking is dangerous in these areas.

What does this sign mean?

ABMW0087RU19

Series of bumps or hollows ahead.

This sign gives advance warning of a series of bumps or hollows ahead. Be prepared to reduce your speed as necessary.

What does this sign mean?

ABMW0088U19

Slippery road ahead.

This sign gives advance warning of the potential danger of slippery road surfaces ahead.

What does this sign mean?
ABMW0089RU19

Unprotected quay, canal or river ahead.

This sign gives advance warning of an unprotected area of water ahead. You should be cautious due to the extreme danger.

What does this sign mean?
ABMW0090RU19

Traffic signals ahead.

This sign gives advance warning of a traffic light controlled junction ahead. This sign is generally found in areas where the lights may not be visible to drivers in good time – for example, following a bend in the road.

What does this sign mean?
ABMW0091RU19

School ahead.

This sign gives advance warning of a school ahead. You should adjust your speed and react accordingly as there may be children in the area.

What does this sign mean?
ABMW0092U19/93U19

School children crossing ahead.

This sign gives advance warning that there may be school children crossing the road ahead, slow down if required and be prepared to stop.

What do these signs together mean?
ABMW0094U19

Beware of children crossing.

These signs are usually displayed in residential areas, and they give advance warning that children might be crossing ahead. You should proceed cautiously and be prepared to stop suddenly.

What does this sign mean?
ABMW0096U19

Possibility of cattle or farm animals ahead.

This sign gives advance warning that there may be cattle or other farm animals on the road ahead. Slow down if required and be prepared to stop.

What does this sign mean?
ABMW0097U19

Possibility of sheep ahead.

This sign gives advance warning that there may be sheep on the road ahead. Slow down if required and be prepared to stop.

What does this sign mean?
ABMW0098U19

Deer or wild animals ahead.

This sign gives advance warning that there may be deer or other wild animals coming onto the roadway. Be prepared to slow down or stop suddenly if required.

What does this sign mean?
ABMW0101RU19

Tunnel ahead.

This sign gives advance warning of a tunnel ahead. You should be aware of the procedures to follow when entering a tunnel – which include keeping a safe distance from the vehicle ahead or removing sunglasses.

What does this sign mean?
ABMW0102RU19

Danger of falling rocks ahead.

This sign gives advance warning that there is a danger of rocks and other debris falling onto the road. Drive with caution.

What does this sign mean?

ABMW0103RU19

Possibility of low flying aircraft.

This sign gives advance warning that there may be low-flying aircraft in the area. Low-flying aircraft can cause distraction due to a sudden loud noise.

What does this sign mean?

ABMW0104RU19

A driver must drive on the left-hand side.

This sign is generally in areas where tourists might be travelling and reminds motorists to drive on the left. These signs are commonly found around airports and ferry ports.

What does this sign mean?

ABMW0105RU19

Tramway crossing ahead.

This sign gives advance warning sign of a tram crossing ahead. You should be prepared to stop and yield to the tram, if required.

What does this sign mean?

ABMW0115U19

Roadworks ahead.

This warning sign tells you that there are roadworks ahead. You should approach with caution and be alert for a change in the road surface, and for the presence of machinery and road workers.

What does this sign mean?

ABMW0117RU19

Slippery road.

This roadworks warning sign tells you that the surface ahead is slippery due to mud or debris and there is an increased risk of skidding.

What does this sign mean?
Road narrows from left.

ABMW0118RU19

This warning sign tells you that there are roadworks up ahead where the road narrows from the left creating a potential hazard.

What does this sign mean?
Road narrows from right.

ABMW0119RU19

Where there are roadworks up ahead, this warning sign tells you that the road narrows from the right creating a potential hazard.

What does this sign mean?
Road narrows on both sides.

ABMW0120RU19

This roadworks warning sign tells you that the road narrows on both sides creating a potential hazard. Be prepared to slow down and drive with extra care.

What does this sign mean?
Flagman ahead.

ABMW0121RU19

This roadworks warning sign tells you that the traffic flow ahead is controlled manually by a flagman. Be aware and follow directions given by the flagman.

What does this sign mean?
Temporary traffic signals ahead.

ABMW0122RU19

This roadworks warning sign tells you that temporary traffic signals are in use ahead. You should prepare to slow down, approach with caution and comply with the signal displayed.

1
2

What does this sign mean?

ABMW0123U19

Two-way traffic.

This warning sign tells you that during roadworks there will be two-way traffic in operation ahead. Continue to drive with extra care.

What does this sign mean?

ABMW0124RU19

Nearside lane of two closed.

This roadworks warning sign tells you that that the nearside (left hand) lane is closed ahead. If you are in this lane you will need to move to the offside (right hand) lane when it is safe to do so.

What does this sign mean?

ABMW0125RU19

Nearside lane of three closed.

This roadworks warning sign tells you that that the nearside (left hand) lane of three is closed up ahead. If you are in this lane you will need to move to the centre (middle) lane when it is safe to do so.

What does this sign mean?

ABMW0127RU19

Offside lane closed ahead.

This roadworks warning sign tells you that that the offside (right hand) lane of three is closed ahead. Drivers in the nearside or centre lanes should be aware that traffic may merge from the right.

What do these signs together mean?

ABMW0134U19

End of detour.

Together these two signs indicate that a detour has ended.

65

What does this sign mean?

ABMW0135RU19

Traffic should cross back to the left-hand lane ahead.

This roadworks warning sign tells you that the course of the road will return to the left ahead. This usually appears after a stretch where traffic was diverted to a right-hand lane.

What does this sign mean?

ABMW0136RU19

Traffic should cross out to the right-hand lane ahead.

This roadworks warning sign tells you that the course of the road will divert to the right ahead.

What does this sign mean?

ABMW0138RU19

End of central reserve or obstruction.

This roadworks warning sign tells you that traffic previously separated by the central reserve or an obstruction will revert to two-way traffic.

Vehicle Markings / Rear Under Run Barriers

What colour rear markings must be fitted to a category C type vehicle?
Red reflector stripes.

C0083R

All category C type vehicles must have reflective markings on the sides and rear. The markings on the rear of the vehicle must be red; those on the sides can be white or amber.

What colour of Retro-reflective material should be used for the markings on the rear of heavy goods vehicles?
C1328AU19

Red.

The rear and side vehicle markings should be made of strips of Retro-reflective Material. Red must be used to the rear of the vehicle. White or yellow must be used on the sides.

Managing Risk

1

2

Forces acting on the vehicle » Air Turbulence

Which type of road user is particularly badly affected by the air-turbulence caused by a passing high-sided vehicle?

CD0093RU19

Pedestrians.

A high-sided vehicle creates air turbulence to the sides and rear of the vehicle, and this turbulence increases with the speed of the vehicle. This affects other road users, and in particular pedestrians, cyclists, motorcyclists and cars towing caravans. The driver should take extra care when passing such road users, to avoid blowing them off course.

What is the effect on a motorcyclist when being overtaken by a large vehicle?

CD0094RU19

The motorcyclist can be blown off course.

A high-sided vehicle creates air turbulence to the sides and rear of the vehicle, and this turbulence increases with the speed of the vehicle. The driver should take extra care when passing motorcyclists, to avoid blowing them off course.

What is the effect on a cyclist when being overtaken by a large vehicle?

It can affect the cyclist's stability.

CD0095RU19

A high-sided vehicle creates air turbulence to the sides and rear of the vehicle, and this turbulence increases with the speed of the vehicle. The driver should take extra care when passing cyclists to avoid affecting their stability.

Which type of vehicle is more likely to be affected by the air-turbulence caused by a passing high-sided vehicle?

CD10U19

Cars towing caravans.

A high-sided vehicle creates air turbulence to the sides and rear of the vehicle, and this turbulence increases with the speed of the vehicle. This affects other road users, and in particular pedestrians, cyclists, motorcyclists and cars towing caravans. The driver should take extra care when passing such road users, to avoid blowing them off course.

Which type of vehicle is more likely to be affected by the air-turbulence caused by a passing high-sided vehicle?

CD11U19

Bicycles.

A high-sided vehicle creates air turbulence to the sides and rear of the vehicle, and this turbulence increases with the speed of the vehicle. This affects other road users, and in particular pedestrians, cyclists, motorcyclists and cars towing caravans. The driver should take extra care when passing such road users, to avoid blowing them off course.

Which type of vehicle is more likely to be affected by the air-turbulence caused by a passing high-sided vehicle?

CD12U19

Motorcycles.

A high-sided vehicle creates air turbulence to the sides and rear of the vehicle, and this turbulence increases with the speed of the vehicle. This affects other road users, and in particular pedestrians, cyclists, motorcyclists and cars towing caravans. The driver should take extra care when passing such road users, to avoid blowing them off course.

1

2

Forces acting on the vehicle

What effect does carrying a load have on a vehicle's braking ability?

It increases the distance required to stop.

ABMW0430RU19

When driving a vehicle which is carrying a load, the driver should be aware that the forces acting on the vehicle will increase the distance required to stop. The driver should allow for this by increasing the distance from the vehicle in front.

What effect does towing a loaded trailer have on stopping ability?

It increases the stopping distance.

ABMW0434RU19

If you are towing a loaded trailer, you need to be aware that your braking distance could be considerably greater, depending on the weight and size of the trailer. The driver should allow for this by increasing the distance from the vehicle in front.

What should a driver be aware of when gaining access to the top of a tanker?
C7U19

That the tank might be slippery.

If you need to gain access to the top of the tanker , be aware that the tanker surface may be slippery. Also that the vehicle is not parked beneath overhead cables, either of these conditions can cause injury or fatality.

When approaching a roundabout, what precaution should the driver take to avoid roll-over?
CD0126RU19

Reduce speed.

A vehicle can become unstable and roll over if it changes direction sharply while being driven too fast. For this reason, when driving a large vehicle, you should slow down on approaching a roundabout to reduce the likelihood of rolling over.

What should a driver be aware of when driving a vehicle that has a high centre of gravity?
CD0131RU19

The vehicle with the higher centre of gravity is more likely to roll over on a bend or roundabout.

If you are driving a large vehicle with a high centre of gravity, you should slow down on bends, corners and roundabouts. The vehicle can become unstable and roll or topple over if it changes direction sharply while being driven too fast.

When a vehicle is stationary on level ground,what force is acting on it?
CD1330U19

Gravity.

When not on an uphill or downhill gradient, and when not in motion, typically the only force acting on a vehicle is the downward pull of gravity.

What effect would cornering forces have on people travelling in a vehicle?
CD1331U19

Thrown towards the outside of the bend.

When cornering a vehicles occupants can be thrown towards the outside of the bend. To ensure passenger comfort and safety, drivers should steer smoothly and avoid taking bends too fast.

What type of energy is stored up by a moving vehicle?
CD1332U19

Kinetic.

Drivers need to be aware that kinetic energy is energy of motion and is stored in a travelling vehicle and may adversely effect the drivers ability to slow down and stop. Be aware that every time a driver doubles their speed they quadruple the amount of kinetic energy, this will considerably increase the breaking distance of the vehicle.

On a downhill gradient, which of the following effects will gravity have?

Increase stopping distances.
CD1333

On a downhill gradient, gravity makes the vehicle's speed increase, therefore stopping distances and the braking effort required to slow the vehicle are also increased.

On an uphill gradient, which of the following effects will gravity have?

Increase the engine power needed to move the vehicle forward.
CD1334

On a gradient, the effect of gravity is to pull the vehicle downhill. For this reason, when travelling uphill, more engine power is required to move the vehicle forward and upward.

Which factor could cause a reduction in a tyre's grip on the road surface?

The condition of suspension components.
CD1335U19

Grip produces traction, which leads to good road holding. Suspension components such as worn shock absorbers or broken springs reduces the amount of grip and could lead to serious loss of control of the vehicle.

1

2

What is the resistance to a change in a vehicle's motion called?

CPC1042AU19

Inertia.

Resistance to movement is called inertia. The opposite of this is momentum – the force that keeps vehicles in motion. Drivers need to be familiar with how the negative effect of these forces impact the vehicles stability.

What is the force that helps to keep a vehicle moving called?

CPC1043AU19

Momentum.

Resistance to movement is called inertia. The opposite of this is momentum – the force that keeps vehicles in motion. Drivers need to be familiar with how the negative effect of these forces impact the vehicles stability.

How does acceleration and braking affect people sitting in a vehicle?

Acceleration pushes passengers back while braking moves them forward.

CPC1045AA

Acceleration will push passengers back, while braking will push them forward. A persons inertia must be overcome in much the same way as the vehicles inertia.

Incidents and Collisions

What should a driver do when involved in an incident where nobody is injured but the vehicles are causing a danger or obstruction on the road? ABMW0611RU19

Take care when moving damaged vehicles and make every effort to warn other traffic.

In a collision where nobody is injured and there is only minor damage to vehicles, the vehicles should be moved to the side of the road to ensure that they do not cause an obstruction or endanger other road users.

What must a driver do when involved in a collision with another driver where there is minor damage done to the vehicles? ABMW0614RA

Stop their vehicle and exchange particulars with the driver of the other vehicle.

If you are involved in a collision you must exchange details with the other driver, no matter how minor the damage is. What may look like minor damage at the time may turn out to be more serious when the vehicles are being repaired. Report the incident to the Gardaí.

What should a driver do if involved in an incident where there is damage to property only? ABMW0615RU19

It is not necessary to report it to the Gardai provided it has been reported to the property owner.

If the incident causes damage to property only and there is a Garda present, it must be reported to the Garda. If there is no Garda present, the owner or the person in charge of the property must be informed. If neither are present then the relevant information must be provided at a Garda Station as soon as possible.

What should a driver do where a person has been injured in a collision? ABMW0616RU19

Move the victim only if there is a risk of fire or further injury.

Never move an injured person at the scene of a collision unless there is a risk of fire or further injury. Moving an injured person could add to their injuries. Trained personnel know best how to attend to injured persons. Call the emergency services (on 999 or 112) or make sure that someone else has called them.

What type of drink should be given to a person who has been injured in a collision?
ABMW0617RU19

No drink should be given.

A person who has been injured in a collision should not be given anything to drink, as this could cause them to choke. Ideally trained personnel should be consulted before attending to an injured person. Call the emergency services (on 999 or 112) or make sure that someone else has called them.

What should a driver do to assist a person who is unconscious following a collision?
ABMW0618RU19

Try to keep the person warm with a blanket or overcoat.

If a person is unconscious following a collision, a driver should try to keep them warm with a blanket or overcoat until the emergency services arrive. Call the emergency services (on 999 or 112) or make sure that someone else has called them.

What is the correct procedure where somebody has been injured in a collision?
ABMW0620RA

Do not move the person unless there is a risk of fire or of the vehicle turning over.

Never move an injured person at the scene of a collision unless there is a risk of fire or further injury. Moving an injured person could make their injuries worse. Call the emergency services (on 999 or 112) or make sure that someone else has called them.

Who should first be contacted where a person has been injured in a collision?
ABMW0621R

The emergency services.

Where somebody has been injured in a collision, it is important to call the emergency services immediately on 999 or 112. Trained emergency services personnel know best how to attend to injured persons.

If a driver is involved in a serious collision with an uninsured motorist, where nobody is injured, who should it be reported to? ABMW0623RU19
The driver's insurance company and the Gardai.

If you are involved in a serious collision, you should always report it to the Gardai and to your insurance company.

What should a driver do if involved in a collision with another vehicle where nobody is injured? ABMW0624RU19
Exchange all relevant details with the other driver.

If a you are involved in a collision with another vehicle where nobody is injured, you should exchange all the relevant details with the other driver – including name, address, vehicle registration, make and model and all insurance details.

What should a driver do if they arrive at the scene of a collision involving a vehicle carrying hazardous materials? ABMW0625RU19
Keep well clear and call the emergency services

If a driver arrives at the scene of a collision involving a vehicle carrying hazardous materials, they should keep well clear of the scene. Call the emergency services on 999 or 112 and give them as much information as you can about the marking labels on the vehicle. You should also warn other road users about the danger. Allow the emergency services to do any rescuing.

A driver has stalled in the middle of an unguarded level crossing and cannot restart the engine. The warning bell is ringing. What should the driver do? BW0046RU19
Walk clear of the crossing and phone the signal operator so that trains can be stopped.

In this situation, the driver and all passengers should get out of the vehicle and immediately use the emergency phone at the crossing to contact the signal operator so that trains can be stopped. If necessary, warn other motorists. Do not return to the vehicle until instructed by the signal operator or emergency services.

1
2

What is the immediate effect of a head-on collision between two cars at speed?

BW0053U19

All persons in each vehicle are thrown violently forward.

In a head-on collision passengers in both vehicles are propelled forwards, and if they are not wearing seatbelts they may go through the windscreen. It is the drivers responsibility to ensure that all passengers under the age of 17 wear seatbelts. Older passengers are themselves responsible for wearing seatbelts.

When should a driver use their hazard warning lights?

BW0073RU19

When the vehicle has broken down.

Use the hazard warning lights to warn other road users of a danger ahead. For example, if a drivers vehicle has broken down and is stopped on the hard shoulder, they should use the vehicles hazard warning lights to warn other road users of their presence.

When should a driver use their vehicle's hazard warning lights?

When causing an unavoidable obstruction.

BW0075RU19

Use the hazard warning lights to warn other road users of a danger ahead. For example, if a drivers vehicle is causing an unavoidable obstruction such as being broken down, they should use the vehicles hazard warning lights to warn other road users of their presence.

When should a driver use their vehicle's hazard warning lights?

When broken down and causing an obstruction.

BW0076RU19

Use the hazard warning lights to warn other road users of a danger ahead. For example, if a drivers vehicle is causing an unavoidable obstruction such as being broken down, they should use the vehicles hazard warning lights to warn other road users of their presence.

In what circumstances may the driver of a truck use the hard shoulder of a motorway?

C6U19

When stopping in an emergency or breakdown.

It is not permissible for the driver of a truck to stop or use the hard shoulder of a motorway except when stopping in an emergency or breakdown. Drivers should familiarise themselves with guidance on motorway emergencies and breakdowns contained in Section 11 in the Rules of the Road.

How should following traffic be warned in the event of an incident on a regional road?
CD0166RU19

By placing a red warning triangle on the road a short distance back from the vehicle involved.

If your vehicle breaks down, or is involved in an incident, place a red warning triangle on the road, far enough from the incident to give following traffic adequate warning.

Under what circumstances should a driver use an emergency red warning triangle?
CD0167RU19

In the event of an incident or breakdown.

If your vehicle breaks down, or is involved in an incident, place a red warning triangle on the road, far enough from the incident to give following traffic adequate warning.

Not knowing the height of your vehicle could lead to an incident with which of the following?
CPC1148U19

Bridges.

It is important to know the height of your vehicle and any load being carried before you start a journey to avoid collision with a bridge.

What is the FIRST thing the driver must do if involved in a collision?
CPC1171AAU19

Stop the vehicle.

Under Irish law, all drivers involved in road traffic collisions firstly must stop their vehicles and remain at the scene for a reasonable period of time. If vehicles are blocking the way posing a danger to other road users the roadway should be marked and the vehicle should be moved as soon as possible.

What is the estimated cost, including lost output, human costs, medical cost, property loss, insurance, and policing, of a road death in Ireland?
CPC1182U19

€2,600,000

Estimated cost of a road death in Ireland reported to and recorded by An Garda Síochana in 2006 was €2,667,600.

If a vehicle breaks down, where should the driver stop?

As far to the left as possible.

CPC1297U19

When a vehicle breaks down it is important to move as far in to the left as possible for the convenience of other road users and the safety of the vehicles occupants

What is the most likely cause of a sudden loss of steering?

A front tyre blowout.

CPC1298AU19

A front tyre blowing out or bursting causes the vehicle to suddenly become difficult to steer or control.

What should the driver do when a front tyre blows out?

CPC1299AU19

Keep a firm hold on the steering wheel.

If your front tyre blows out: keep a firm hold on the steering wheel, be aware of anything on your left side, signal left and try to steer a steady course to the left.

What must a driver do first if involved in a collision?

CPC1300AU19

Stop the vehicle.

If you are involved in an accident, you must stop the vehicle and stay at the scene for a reasonable time. This is Irish law.

When should a driver use hazard warning lights?

CPC1301AU19

To warn road users of a vehicle breakdown.

When your vehicle has broken down, switch on your hazard warning lights and parking lights. This warns other road users of a breakdown.

In the event of an engine compartment fire, what action should a driver take?

CPC1302U19

Spray foam through the grill.

Where fire breaks out in an engine compartment it is important to take safe steps to put it out. Avoid lifting the bonnet or grill as this may expose you to flames. If tackling the fire the driver should direct foam spray through the grill.

What must a driver do first if involved in a accident?

CPC1303AU19

Stop the vehicle.

If you are involved in an accident, you must stop the vehicle and stay at the scene for a reasonable time. This is Irish law.

What is the first thing a driver should do if their vehicle breaks down on a railway level crossing?

CPC1305AU19

Phone the railway controller to alert them to the danger.

If you breakdown or get stuck on a level crossing, make sure that everybody gets out and gets clear of the railway line then use the phone provided to contact the signal operator or warn of the danger as best you can.

What is the quickest way to warn other traffic of a crash?

CPC1307U19

Use hazard lights.

If you arrive at the scene of a crash find a safe place to stop so that you don't endanger yourself or others, warn other road users of the incident by using hazard lights.

When should a driver should use hazard warning lights?

CPC1309U19

When a vehicle has broken down.

When a vehicle has broken down it is important to warn other road users of the vehicles position so that they may take appropriate action. An important first step is to switch on the hazard warning lights.

What should the driver do if a front tyre blows out?

CPC1312AU19

Keep a firm hold on the steering wheel.

If your front tyre blows out: keep a tight hold on the steering wheel, be aware of anything on your left side, signal left and try to steer a steady course to the left side, slow down gradually and avoid hard braking, try to stop the vehicle under control.

What should a driver avoid doing when a front tyre blows out? CPC1314AU19
Harsh braking.

Hard and sudden braking will make the vehicle more unstable, so do not do it with reduced road grip. If your front tyre blows out: keep a firm hold on the steering wheel, be aware of anything on your left side, signal left and try to steer a steady course to the left side, slow down gradually and avoid hard braking, try to stop the vehicle under control as far to the left as you can, switch on the hazard warning lights, use a red warning triangle except on a motorway .

In order to inform the emergency services of a crash what telephone number should be called? CPC1316U19
112

If a driver arrives at or is involved in a crash it may be essential to obtain the assistance of the emergency services as a matter of urgency. The common European emergency number is 112 however in Ireland you may also use 999.

When calling for help on an emergency telephone on the motorway, who does the call go to? CPC1317U19
The Gardaí.

The emergency telephones at the side of a motorway are linked directly to An Garda Síochána in order for them to respond appropriately as soon as possible. The Gardaí know precisely the location of each call using these phones.

Where an injured person is discovered lying in the road, when should they be moved? CPC1322U19
If the person needs CPR.

If a person discovered lying in the road is not breathing it may be essential to move them in order to safely carry out emergency CPR. It may also be necessary to move them under other circumstances but an urgent assessment of the situation should be carried out first.

When dealing with crash victims, remember A B C. What does A stand for? CPC1324U19
Airway.

In assessing a crash victims vital signs the following basic procedure should be used First check the victims Airway is clear, then check they are Breathing and then check their Circulation (ABC)

When dealing with crash victims, remember A B C. What does C stand for?

CPC1326U19

Circulation.

In assessing a crash victims vital signs the following basic procedure should be used First check the victims Airway is clear, then check they are Breathing and then check their Circulation (ABC)

What is good basic first aid for a person who has been burned?

CPC1329U19

Remove clothing covering the burn.

When a person has been burned firstly check the person for shock, then try to cool the burn if you can. Try to find water or other liquid that is clean, cold and non-toxic to pour on it. The cool liquid may cool the affected area down and reduce damage. The person should be advised to seek medical advice as soon as possible.

At a crash scene, where a persons arm or leg is bleeding but not broken, what basic first aid action should be taken?

CPC1331U19

Raise arm or leg to reduce blood flow.

Where a crash victim is discovered at the scene of an incident and the persons arm or leg is bleeding but not broken, raise the arm or leg to reduce the blood flow. If appropriate the person should be advised to seek medical attention.

When dealing with crash victims, remember A B C. What does B stand for?

CPC1333U19

Breathing.

In assessing a crash victims vital signs the following basic procedure should be used First check the victims Airway is clear, then check they are Breathing and then check their Circulation (ABC)

When dealing with accident victims, remember A B C. What does C stand for?

CPC1334U19

Circulation.

In assessing a crash victims vital signs the following basic procedure should be used First check the victims Airway is clear, then check they are Breathing and then check their Circulation (ABC)

What should a driver do if their vehicle catches fire while driving? CPC1336U19
Pull over and stop safely as soon as possible.

If your vehicle catches fire whilst driving , stop as soon as it is safe to do so. Evacuate the vehicle with care for the occupants safety. Call emergency services. Do not open the engine compartment as the rush of air could fan the flames.

What should a driver do if they think there is a fire inside the engine compartment? CPC1337AU19
Stop safely and as soon as possible.

If your vehicle catches fire whilst driving, stop as soon as it is safe to do so. Evacuate the vehicle with care for the occupants safety. Call emergency services. Do not open the engine compartment as the rush of air could fan the flames.

While driving through a tunnel with smoke or fire coming from the vehicle in front, what should a driver do first? CPC1339U19
Stop and turn off the engine.

If there is smoke or fire in a vehicle in front of you: Stop your vehicle safely and switch off the engine, Leave your vehicle immediately, Go to an emergency station and phone the tunnel operator, Leave the tunnel from the nearest exit. Do not pass.

What should a driver do first in the event of their vehicle breaking down?
Switch on the hazard warning lights. CPC1396U19

If your vehicle breaks down you should firstly switch on your hazard warning lights to alert other road users. Place a warning triangle behind the vehicle (except on a motorway). Assess the situation and call for assistance if required.

How many road deaths were there in Ireland in 2017? CPC1409BU19
158.

In 2017, there were 158 road deaths in Ireland (provisional report). This number continues to fall thanks to the improved behaviour of all road users. By taking personal responsibility for your own behaviour on the roads, you can help further improve these figures.

What is the benefit of driving with anticipation and awareness?
A reduction in accident risk.

CPC1461U19

By driving with anticipation and awareness of surroundings, you reduce your risk of being involved in an accident.

What should a driver do in a hi-jack or hostage situation?
Obey orders.

CPC1477AU19

Do not make the situation worse. The safest course of action is to obey any orders given by the person making the threat.

Lights

Why is it important to ensure that the vehicle headlights are correctly aligned?
To enable the driver to see properly.

ABMW0633RU19

A driver should ensure their headlights are properly aligned so as not to dazzle oncoming drivers and also to see properly themselves.

In general, how frequently should a vehicle's lights be checked?
Daily before driving.

ABMW0636RU19

A driver is responsible for their vehicles roadworthiness and they should check it daily before driving. Among the checks they should make are that all the lights are clean and in working order.

What effect can a broken lens have on headlights?
It can reduce and distort the beam.

ABMW0637RU19

A driver is responsible for their vehicles roadworthiness and they should check it at regular intervals. Among the checks they should make are that all the lights are in working order. If they find defects in the lights, such as a broken lens, they should have them repaired or replaced as soon as possible.

A driver wishes to drive at night, but the off-side (right-hand side) headlight bulb is blown. What should the driver do?

ABMW0638RU19

Not drive until the bulb is replaced.

A driver is responsible for their vehicles roadworthiness and they should check it at regular intervals. Drivers must not drive on the road unless their vehicles headlights are in good working order, adjusted properly and clean.

Is it permissible to drive a vehicle on a public road when the brake lights are not working?

ABMW0642RU19

No, it is never permitted to be driven.

A driver must always ensure that their vehicles brake-lights are clean and working correctly before driving on a public road. Never drive a vehicle when the brake lights are not working properly.

What does this light mean?

ABMW0643RU19

The battery is not charging.

If the battery warning light comes on whilst driving, it means there is some kind of problem with the electrical charging system of the vehicle and the battery is not being charged properly. The driver should get this checked by a professional as soon as possible. It is important to understand the meaning of your vehicles warning lights, information on which can be found in the vehicles handbook.

What does this light mean?

ABMW0644RU19

The high-beam headlights are switched on.

All vehicles are fitted with warning lights to alert the driver to different things. This light comes on when the full beam headlights are turned on. It is important to understand the meaning of your vehicles warning lights, information on which can be found in the vehicles handbook.

What does this light mean?

ABMW0645U19

Low engine oil level.

If the engine oil warning light comes on, it means that the engine oil level/ pressure has dropped. You should not drive the vehicle until the problem is fixed. If the light comes on while driving, pull over and stop in a safe place as soon as possible. It is important to understand the meaning of your vehicles warning lights, information on which can be found in the vehicles handbook.

What does this light mean?
ABMW0646RU19

Directional indicator on.

All vehicles are fitted with warning lights to alert you to different things. This light tells you that the directional indicator is on. If this light is still on after you have completd your manoeuvre, cancel it to avoid misleading other road users. It is important to understand the meaning of your vehicles warning lights, information on which can be found in the vehicles handbook.

What should a driver do if the right-hand headlight bulb fails when driving at night?
BW0028RU19

Have the bulb replaced immediately.

Vehicles (except motorcycles) are required by law to have right and left headlights. Faulty lights should be repaired immediately. A vehicle with only one headlight can cause a hazard to other road users or be mistaken for a motorcycle.

What effect do the hazard warning lights have on the brake lights?
BW0072RU19

They have no effect.

The hazard lights work independently of the other lights on the vehicle (except the direction indicators), and have no effect on the brake lights. Use the hazard warning lights to warn other road users of a danger ahead, when your vehicle is broken down and causing an obstruction, or when you needs to slow down sharply on a motorway.

What lighting must be on a two-axle car-trailer?
BW0077RU19

Indicators, brake lights, rear number plate light, red reflectors and rear tail lights.

All vehicles, including trailers, must have rear indicators, brake lights, a rear number plate light, red reflectors and rear tail lights.

1
2

Load Handling

How does the driver know the vehicle's total load-carrying capacity?

By referring to the vehicle manufacturer's specification. ABMW0628RU19

Design Gross Vehicle Weight is the term used by manufacturers for the weight of the vehicle together with the maximum load it is designed to carry. Drivers must understand the carrying capacity of their vehicle. Overloading your vehicle will make it more difficult to control, and its an offence.

What determines the maximum allowed towing capacity of a vehicle?

The manufacturer's specifications. ABMW0629U19

The maximum weight that your vehicle can safely tow is specified by the manufacturer, and is usually set out in the drivers handbook for the vehicle, and in some cases on a plate attached to the vehicle. This is the safe towing limit for the vehicle and you should not exceed it.

What effect can overloading a vehicle have on its road-holding?

The load can make the vehicle more difficult to control. ABMW0630U19

Overloading your vehicle will make it more difficult to control. Remember: its an offence to overload a vehicle.

What would be the effect of overloading a vehicle with passengers or goods? ABMW0631RU19

It would reduce the driver's ability to control the vehicle.

Overloading your vehicle will make it more difficult to control, and will increase the risk of a collision

What effect could an unevenly distributed load have on a vehicle? ABMW0632RU19

It could make the vehicle unstable while turning.

When loading a vehicle you should ensure that the load is distributed evenly. An unevenly distributed load may change the vehicles centre of gravity and this could affect the braking and steering.

What effect does increasing the load have on the vehicle's braking ability? C0041A

It increases the normal stopping distance required.

In general, a heavier load makes a truck more difficult to stop and increases the required stopping distance.

How does air suspension affect a vehicle's carrying capacity, compared to that of a vehicle with conventional suspension? C0042R

It allows extra weight to be carried.

Air suspension (road-friendly suspension) provides the vehicle with an even load height, whether it is empty or fully laden. It allows for extra weight to be carried by the vehicle, and helps to protect fragile goods in transit.

What additional precautions should be taken when transporting bulk liquid? C0043U19

The tanks should be sectioned off.

Where possible, vehicles that carry bulk liquids should have the tank divided up into sections or have baffle plates installed to reduce the wave effect and help the driver to slow or stop the vehicle smoothly.

How should a load of loose dusty material be carried? C0044R

It should be covered with a tarpaulin or sheeting.

When dusty material, such as sand or grain, is carried, the load should be covered with a tarpaulin or sheeting to avoid the load being lost by blowing off the vehicle and creating a hazard or nuisance for other road users.

What should a driver ensure when carrying hazardous materials? C0045R

That they comply with the regulations on the conveyance of dangerous substances by road.

If you are driving a vehicle that is carrying hazardous materials, you are responsible for taking all the appropriate precautions to ensure public safety. The driver must be qualified to transport the specific material and the vehicle must be equipped with the relevant safety equipment and labels.

1
2

What should a driver of a tipper truck be aware of when tipping a load from their vehicle?
C0047R

Overhead cables and power lines.

Before raising the tipper body, check to see that there are no overhead cables or power lines that could be touched by the raised body. Failure to make this check could prove fatal.

Why should ropes not be used to tie down a load of steel girders?
C0055RU19

Because they may wear and snap.

Sharp edges on steel girders can cause the ropes to fray and snap, with the result that a load becomes insecure. If a load has sharp edges, drivers should use web straps with suitable sleeves to protect the webbing from the sharp edges.

Why should the cargo area of a truck carrying loose sand be covered?
C0056RU19

To prevent the sand from blowing away.

When dusty material, such as sand or grain is carried, the load should be covered with a tarpaulin or sheeting to avoid it being blown off the vehicle and creating a hazard or nuisance for other road users. Be aware that the driver is responsible for ensuring the safe carriage of the load.

Who can be held responsible if a truck is found to be overloaded?
C0061R

Both the driver and the owner.

Both the owner and the driver can be held responsible if a goods vehicle is found to be overloaded on a public road.

Who is responsible for making sure that a truck's load is secure during a journey?
C0062RU19

The driver.

It is the driver's responsibility to ensure that the vehicle has been loaded correctly, securely and within its various legal limits. The driver should also check their load at regular intervals as it may settle or move during the journey, with possible damage to or loss of the load.

What action should a driver take if they are out making an urgent delivery and notice that some of the twist locks or container securing devices are broken?

C0064RU19

They should not drive until the twist-locks have been repaired or replaced.

Drivers are responsible for the security of their loads. If the twist locks are defective on a container-carrying vehicle, the container could fall off the vehicle particularly when changing speed or direction. Continuing to drive in these circumstances is dangerous could result in serious injury and or damage to property.

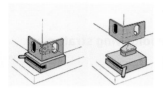

What are twist locks used to secure?

C0065RU19

A steel cargo container onto a vehicle or trailer.

Twist locks are used to secure a steel container to a flat-bed or skeletal trailer. Drivers must make sure that the twist locks are in good condition and are in the unlocked position when the container is being lifted on or off the trailer. Drivers must ensure that they are in the locked position before commencing and at regular intervals throughout the journey.

1

2

How should timber loads be loaded on a vehicle?

C0066RU19

Against the headboard and the weight evenly distributed.

Timber loads should be placed against the headboard where possible , and the weight distributed evenly between the axles to ensure stability. In general, they should be secured with strong chains or similar devices. These should be placed at points where the load is rigid.

What effect will cornering force have on a heavy load when a vehicle goes around a bend ?

C0069RU19

It will cause the vehicle's load to be thrown towards the outside of the bend.

On the approach to bends, drivers must safely adjust the vehicle's speed to suit road and traffic conditions. If a goods vehicle takes a bend too fast, the cornering force will cause the load to be thrown towards the outside of the bend. If the load is not properly secured, it may move and can even fall from the vehicle. If the road is slippery this may even cause the vehicle to skid.

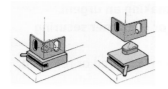

How should an ISO cargo container be secured to a flat-bed or skeletal trailer?

C0071RU19

With twist locks.

Twist locks are used to secure a steel container to a flat-bed or skeletal trailer. Drivers must make sure that the twist locks are in good condition and are in the unlocked position when the container is being lifted on or off the trailer. Drivers must ensure that they are in the locked position before commencing a journey and check them at regular intervals.

To secure a load in a box body truck, which of the following strategies should be used?

C1324U19

Tightly pack the boxes together.

Tightly packed boxes are less likely to move than those that are loosely packed. This enhances load security and safety as well as vehicle stability.

What is a risk of driving an overloaded vehicle?

CD0146RU19

The vehicle's stability can be affected.

The effects of overloading a vehicle include damage to the road surfaces, damage to the vehicle itself, and loss of stability in the vehicle, possibly leading to a serious incident. Overloading is against the law, punishable by fines and imprisonment.

When a driver is physically carrying a load, where on the driver's body should the load be positioned?

CPC1226AAU19

Waist.

When physically carrying a load a person should keep the load and their arms close to their waist. Hug it as close to the body as possible. This will help to reduce the risk of injury.

When lifting a load how should a driver stand?
CPC1227AU19

With feet apart, with one leg slightly forward of the other.

In order to reduce the risk of injury whilst lifting a load drivers should place their feet about hip distance apart with one leg slightly forward to help keep their balance.

When lifting a load, what is the best posture for a driver to maintain?
Straight back but inclined forwards.
CPC1228U19

Keeping the normal curve of your back while lifting may help to reduce the risk of injury.

When carrying a heavy package and needing to change direction what should a driver do?
CPC1229AAU19

Move with the feet.

Where a driver needs to change direction whilst carrying a heavy package they should avoid twisting at the waist and move with their feet, instead. This will help to reduce the risk of injury.

Where a driver using a well maintained handling aid needs to move a heavy load on an uneven surface, up to what percentage of the load weight may be needed to move it?
CPC1243U19

10%.

Moving an object over an uneven surface, the force needed to start the load moving could increase up to 10% of the load weight. Soft ground may require even greater effort.

When drivers are handling goods what area of the body is most at risk of injury or wear and tear?
CPC1440U19

Back.

The main concern with manual handling is the increased risk of injury or wear and tear to the back.

What is the term used to describe the science of fitting the job to the worker?
CPC1441U19

Ergonomics.

The RST-CMT-08, CPC Manual defines ergonomics as the science of fitting the job to the worker and adapting the work environment to the needs of humans.

What is the first step in lifting safely?
CPC1442U19

Assessing the load.

To make a safe and successful lift a person should first assess the load and determine its weight, its edges and surface, then decide how to hold it.

Where should passengers' heavy luggage be stored?
D0037RU19

In the luggage compartment.

Bus drivers are responsible for the safety and comfort of all of the passengers, and for the vehicle. Store heavy luggage in the luggage compartment. Heavy luggage in the passenger compartment could pose a danger to the passengers in the event of any sudden braking or change in direction.

1
2

Load Security

With regard to the load they are carrying what should a driver ensure?

That it does not cause danger or nuisance to other road users.   C0037AAU19

You must make sure that your load is safely and securely loaded, and that the load is evenly distributed over the axles. Make sure also that the load does not pose any danger or inconvenience to other road users.

How might an unevenly distributed load affect a truck?

The truck's stability is adversely affected.   C0039

You must make sure that your load is safely and securely loaded, and that the load is evenly distributed over the axles. An insecure or unbalanced load, or one that is too heavy, can compromise the safety and stability of the vehicle.

What effect does sharp braking have on a loosely secured load?

The load tends to go to the front of the vehicle.   C0040

You must make sure that your load is safely and securely loaded. If you brake or change direction suddenly, an insecure load can shift or fall off, causing the vehicle to lose stability and creating a hazard for other road users.

Who is responsible for making sure that a truck's load is secure before undertaking a journey?

C0062RAU19

The driver.

It is the drivers responsibility to know how a vehicle has been loaded and how the load has been secured. You should also check your load at regular intervals, as it may settle or move during the journey, thereby causing the straps or chains to loosen.

How should a load of steel scaffolding poles be secured?

C0068RAU19

Secured firmly with strong chains or similar devices.

Steel scaffolding poles should be loaded against the headboard of the trailer and secured with strong chains or similar devices. The driver should stop at regular intervals during the journey to check the tension of the chains.

Preparing for a journey

What should a driver do if condensation is affecting the vehicle's windows?

BW0010RU19

Dry the windows with a cloth and then use the demister system.

Make sure the windows are clear and clean at all times so that the driver can see the road and traffic conditions all around. Condensation on the window can seriously impair your ability to make proper observations. Drivers should familiarise themselves with how to correctly set the vehicle's ventilation system in order to keep the windows clear.

How can sunlight affect visibility in a car with grimy windows?

BW0011RU19

It can seriously reduce visibility.

It is essential that all vehicle windows are clear and clean at all times so that drivers can see road and traffic conditions all around. Dirty windows are a particular hazard when the sun is low in the sky. Dirty windows also decrease visibility during hours of twilight and darkness.

What should a driver do before entering a tunnel?

BW0035RU19

Check that the height of the vehicle is suitable for the tunnel.

Drivers need to know the height of their vehicle and the load being carried, and plan their route accordingly. They should always read the road ahead and watch for warning signs. These may relate to tunnels, low bridges or car park entrances.

What should a driver do before starting a journey on which they will encounter a tunnel?

BW0036RU19

Check the tunnel height before starting the journey.

Drivers need to know the height of their vehicle and the load being carried, and plan their route accordingly. They should always read the road ahead and watch for warning signs. These may relate to tunnels, low bridges or car park entrances.

A driver transporting a long load of 25 metres in length plans a journey which will take place entirely on designated roads. Which of the following permits is required? C1326U19

Garda permit.

A Garda permit is required for a journey which takes place entirely on designated roads, by using a vehicle with a load which exceeds the regulation length, but which does not exceed 27.4 metres in length or 4.3 metres in width or 4.65 metres in height.

A driver transporting a long load of 28 metres in length plans a journey which will take place entirely on designated roads. Which of the following permits is required? C1327U19

A Local Authority permit for each local authority area passed through.

A Local Authority permit is required for each Local Authority area the vehicle is passing through. The permit is required while carrying a load which exceeds a length of more than 27.4 metres or 4.3 metres in width or 4.65 metres in height.

1
2

When estimating the time for a journey, what should a driver allow extra time for? CD0034R

Driving during 'rush-hour' traffic.

A journey will nearly always take longer than expected because of traffic jams, road works, adverse weather conditions, and so on. A driver should understand this and allow sufficient time to complete the journey in a safe manner.

When estimating the time for a journey, what should a driver allow extra time for? CD0035R

Mandatory rest breaks.

A journey will nearly always take longer than expected because of traffic jams, road works, adverse weather conditions, and so on. A driver should understand this and allow sufficient time to complete the journey in a safe manner.

A driver comes to a bridge with a weight limit that is lower than their vehicle's weight. What should the driver do? CD0038U19

Turn around and find an alternative route.

Drivers must never exceed the stated weight limit. If a driver encounters a restriction lower than the weight of the vehicle they must not proceed. They should take an alternative route. Good journey planning by drivers will improve road safety by preventing this situation from arising.

When driving a low-loader vehicle with a wide load, what should a driver allow for? CD0121RU19

Narrow bridges.

A low loader is a semi-trailer used to transport heavy oversized vehicles. When loaded, it may be higher, wider and lower than a standard vehicle. If you are driving such a vehicle, you should be aware of these extra hazards and plan your route accordingly, avoiding, where necessary, obstacles such as humpback or narrow bridges and overhead cables.

When driving a car-transporter, what should a driver plan ahead for?

Low railway bridges. CD0124RAU19

The driver of a car transporter should be aware of the extra height of the vehicle when it is loaded with the cars, the instability of the vehicle when only the top deck is loaded, and, on articulated car transporters, the fact that front overhang does not follow the line of the cab when turning.

How can sunlight affect visibility in a vehicle with grimy windows?

It can reduce visibility. CD0140U19

A grimy or greasy windscreen can impair a drivers ability to see the road ahead and compromise their ability to react and respond to changing conditions. It is essential to ensure that all windows are clean. If you are adversely affected by sunlight consider using sunglasses.

What should a driver do when the exterior mirrors are covered with a film of dirt or grime? CD0144RU19

Stop the vehicle and clean the mirrors before continuing.

A driver should always ensure that they can see clearly in their exterior mirrors. If drivers discover that mirrors are dusty or dirty, they should be cleaned before continuing to provide maximum visibility of the road.

Protective Clothing

Who is responsible for supplying any Personal Protective Equipment (PPE) required by the driver?
CD1303U19

The employer.

The regulations require employers to provide Personal Protective Equipment (PPE) to their employees where there is a risk to their health and safety.

To ensure that Personal Protective Equipment (PPE) is maintained in serviceable condition, when should it be inspected?
CD1304U19

Before initial use during each work shift.

Personal Protective Equipment (PPE) is provided to help protect the wearer from a wide range of risks and hazards whilst working. The regulations require that PPE is serviceable and fit for purpose. Regular inspections ensure that this equipment is maintained in this condition. Therefore it is essential that it is carefully checked before starting work.

1

2

Where Personal Protective Equipment (PPE) is found to be defective or damaged on inspection when must it be repaired or replaced?
CD1305U19

Before initial use on each work shift.

The regulations require that personal protective equipment is serviceable and fit for purpose whenever it is required. As such, if it is found to be defective, it should be replaced or repaired before work begins.

Safety Equipment

In general, how should children under 3 years of age be secured in a vehicle?

BW0124U19

They should always be secured in the correct child seat.

Safety belts are designed mainly for adults and older children. Children under 3 years of age must be restrained in an appropriate child restraint system. Warning; Never use a rearward facing child car seat in a seat protected by an active frontal airbag.

Can a child under the age of 3 years be carried unrestrained in the vehicle's front passenger seat.

BW0125RU19

No, an infant must always be restrained in the correct child seat.

Generally, children must never travel unrestrained in a vehicle. Children under 3 years of age must be restrained in an appropriate child restraint system. Warning ; Never use a rearward facing child car seat in a seat protected by an active frontal airbag.

What should a driver ensure when carrying out an inspection under a raised tipper body?

C0046R

That the body is supported by props.

Never carry out an inspection under a raised tipper body unless the body is properly supported by props. The prop used should be strong enough to hold the structure in place if the hydraulic raising system malfunctions.

When towing a trailer a warning device or flag must be attached to a drawbar when it exceeds what length?

C0082RU19

1.5 metres.

To draw attention to a tow bar between a vehicle and trailer a warning device such as a white flag of at least thirty centimetres squared must be attached to the towbar where the distance between the vehicles exceed 1.5 metres. Please note: The maximum permitted distance between a drawing vehicle and a trailer is 4.5 metres.

What is the purpose of rear under-run barriers? C0084
To prevent cars from going under the body of the vehicle from the rear.

Rear under-run barriers are protection barriers attached to the rear of a truck, trailer or semi-trailer. They are designed to prevent small vehicles such as cars and light vans from going under the truck if it stops or decelerates suddenly, and thus help to avoid or reduce serious or fatal injury.

Which of the following vehicles are required to be fitted with rear underrun protective devices? C1329U19
All vehicles up to 2,500 kg.

In general, goods vehicles, trailers and semi-trailers having a design gross vehicle weight exceeding 3,500 kg must be fitted with a rear underrun protective device.

Which of the following rear underrun protective devices would pass a vehicle inspection? C1330
The distance between the device and the road surface is 550mm.

Rear underrun protective devices must not increase the overall width of the vehicle when fitted.

What easily determines the contents of fire extinguishers? CPC1469AU19
The coloured label.

The content of a fire extinguisher can easily be determined by the coloured label on the extinguisher. In combating a fire it is important that the correct type of fire extinguisher is used.

What safety equipment must be carried on a bus or minibus? D0038R
A fire extinguisher and first aid kit.

All buses or minibuses must carry an advance warning triangle, a fire extinguisher and a first-aid kit. These are the basic essentials that may be needed in an emergency situation, such as a collision.

1
2

Vehicle Safety and Technical Checks

Which of the following statements is true in relation to tyre pressure and driving on a motorway? ABMW0487RU19

The driver should ensure that tyre pressure is correct, in line with the manufacturer's recommendations.

The driver should ensure that the tyre pressure of their vehicle is correct at all times. Correct tyre pressure is especially important when travelling long distances, on motorways and at speed.

How would a driver know that a brake-light bulb is not working? ABMW0640RU19

By standing at the rear of the vehicle and checking as another person presses the brake pedal.

In order for a driver to know that the rear brake lights are working correctly, they should stand at the rear of the vehicle and check that the brake lights come on while another person presses the brakes.

What should a driver do if a system warning light lights up on the dashboard of their vehicle whilst driving? ABMW0650RU19

Stop and check the problem.

If a system warning light lights up while you are driving, you should stop in a safe place as soon as possible and investigate the problem before deciding what action to take. It is important to understand the meaning of your vehicles warning lights, information on which can be found in the vehicles handbook.

What should a driver do if a red system warning light lights up on the dashboard of their vehicle? ABMW0651RU19

Stop and investigate the cause.

If a red system warning light comes on while you are driving, you should stop in a safe place as soon as possible and investigate the problem before deciding what action to take. It is important to understand the meaning of your vehicles warning lights, information on which can be found in the vehicles handbook.

What is the purpose of the red reflectors at the rear of a vehicle?

ABMW0652RU19

They reflect light at night to make other road users aware of the vehicle.

Motor vehicles are fitted with red reflectors to make it easier to be seen by other road users. Drivers should keep reflectors clean, intact and check them by shining a light on them to make sure that they are working effectively. Whilst driving, drivers should be cautious as red reflectors may be an indication of both parked/stationery or moving vehicles ahead.

If, when driving along, the driver notices that the engine power is lower than normal, what should they do?

Have the vehicle checked by a competent person.

ABMW0664RU19

If the driver notices that the vehicle seems underpowered when driving, this could present a number of problems, e.g. lack of power when overtaking. The driver should have it checked by a competent person as soon as possible as there may be a number of causes, some of which may deteriorate further.

While driving, a driver notices a strong smell of fuel. What should they do?

ABMW0672RU19

Stop where safe and investigate.

A strong smell of fuel is usually an indication that something is wrong, and drivers should stop and investigate as soon as possible. Leaking or spilling petrol can be dangerous because it is so combustible, and leaking diesel fuel can make the road very slippery.

While driving, the driver notices the vehicle temperature gauge showing red. What should they do?

ABMW0677RU19

Stop in a safe place and have the problem investigated.

Many vehicles are fitted with various warning lights and gauges. A warning light or a red zone on a temperature gauge means the engine is starting to overheat and the vehicle should not be driven until the problem is rectified. Refer to the vehicle handbook for further information and guidance or seek advice from a competent person.

What should a driver do if they notice steam rising from the engine compartment?
ABMW0678RU19

Stop where safe and investigate the cause.

If a driver notices steam rising from the engine compartment of their vehicle, they should stop where safe and only investigate the cause once it has cooled down. Do not remove a radiator or header tank cap when the engine is hot. Steam rising from the engine is an indication that the engine is overheating and it should not continue to be driven. Refer to the vehicle handbook for further information and guidance or seek advice from a competent person.

If a driver notices that structural parts of their vehicle's body have been affected by rust, what should they do?
ABMW0680RU19

Have it repaired by a competent repair shop.

Over time vehicles may become affected by rust to various degrees. Drivers should inspect their vehicles periodically and if they find signs of rust they should have it assessed and repaired if necessary to prevent further deterioration. A weakened vehicle structure may have serious consequences in the event of a collision.

After changing a wheel on a vehicle, which of the following should be checked soon afterwards?
ABMW0694RU19

The wheel nuts.

After changing a wheel on a vehicle it is recommended to check the wheel nuts after a short period of driving to ensure they are still properly secured.

In general, how often should a driver check the tyre pressure of a vehicle?
ABMW0696RU19

Regularly.

Drivers have a legal responsibility to make sure that their vehicle is roadworthy. To do this, they should carry out regular, weekly and periodic checks, including a weekly tyre pressure check. Incorrectly inflated tyres may cause vehicle instability, uneven tyre wear and longer stopping distances.

What is the main reason for maintaining the correct tyre pressures?
To help provide optimum road holding. ABMW0697RU19

The vehicle manufacturer specifies the pressure to which tyres on a vehicle should be inflated. This is the pressure that gives the best performance in road holding, efficient braking and fuel consumption. Some manufacturers specify different pressures for front and rear tyres.

A fault in which component may lead to uneven or excessive tyre wear?
Suspension. ABMW0698RU19

If a vehicle has a worn suspension it may lead to uneven or excessive tyre wear. If drivers notice that their tyres are unevenly worn, they should investigate the reason and have it repaired by a competent person.

What can be affected by driving on under-inflated tyres?
Fuel consumption. ABMW0699RU19

Incorrect tyre pressure adversely affects many of a vehicles systems, including brakes, suspension and steering. In particular, under-inflated tyres can increase the vehicles fuel consumption. Check tyre pressures regularly and ensure they are inflated as per manufacturer's recommendations.

When should tyre pressure be checked? ABMW0700RU19
When the tyres are cold.

Drivers should check the tyre pressure in their vehicle at least once a week and before commencing a long journey. For accuracy, do this when the tyres are cold and using a reliable gauge. Tyres should always be inflated according to the vehicle manufacturers guidelines, information on which can be found in the vehicle handbook.

During a weekly check, a driver notices a badly worn front tyre. What should the driver do? ABMW0702RU19
Have the worn tyre replaced.

The tyres are the vehicles only contact with the road, the area of contact is small and, if worn, will not grip properly and safely. The quality of the tyres on a vehicle is an important factor in the vehicles road holding and braking ability. Drivers should check their tyres regularly and if they notice that a tyre is badly worn, they should replace it immediately. Whilst the minimum legal tread depth for tyres on most vehicles is 1.6mm (1mm for motorcycles), drivers should replace a tyre before it becomes this worn.

What effect could hitting or mounting the kerb have on a vehicle's tyres?

It could damage the sidewalls. ABMW0703RU19

Drivers should avoid hitting or mounting the kerb as it causes damage to the sidewalls of the tyre. The damage caused could cause the tyre to blow-out later. If this happens at high speed the driver may lose control of the vehicle with dangerous consequences.

What does worn tread along the edge of the inside of a tyre suggest?

Steering alignment may be faulty. ABMW0704RU19

If a driver notice the inside edge of the tyre is worn, this may indicate a problem with the steering alignment. This is a potentially dangerous problem, and should be fixed by a competent person as soon as possible. Failure to do so may result in a blow-out and loss of control of the vehicle.

With regard to tyres, what should a driver do before starting a long journey?

ABMW0706RU19

Check the tyres are inflated to normal air pressure.

It is important to check the tyre pressure before starting a long journey as incorrect air pressure can adversely affect many of the vehicles systems, including brakes, steering, suspension and fuel consumption. Tyres should always be inflated according to the vehicle manufacturers guidelines, information on which can be found in the vehicle handbook.

Under what circumstances would a driver increase the air pressure in the tyres?

ABMW0707RU19

When taking a journey with additional passengers.

Before starting a journey with extra passengers or loads, drivers should check the air pressure and when they inflate the tyres, they should increase the vehicles tyre pressures in accordance with the vehicle manufacturers recommended tyre pressure. This information can be found in the vehicle manufacturers handbook.

What should the driver do to secure the vehicle when changing a front nearside (left-hand side) wheel?
ABMW0710RU19

Ensure that the vehicle cannot roll when jacked up.

If a driver has to change a front nearside (left-hand side) wheel, make sure to do it in a safe place on level ground. Take care, wear high visibility vest/jacket, use a warning triangle and hazard warning lights as appropriate. The vehicle should be secured by applying the parking brake (hand brake), switching off the engine, engaging a low gear and using a wheel chock if necessary. If unfamiliar with how to change a wheel seek assistance from a competent person.

What is the most common cause of heavy steering?
ABMW0714RU19

Under-inflated tyres.

Heavy steering is when a driver needs to use more effort than usual to turn the steering wheel, this may be as a direct result of under-inflated tyres. Check your tyre pressures but be aware there may be other causes of heavy steering such as low power steering fluid level. Seek advice from a competent person and have this investigated immediately.

Which of the following is a driver required to keep in good condition?
ABMW25U19

Seatbelts.

Drivers are responsible for their vehicles roadworthiness and should check them at regular intervals. Among the checks they should make are that all the seatbelts (drivers and passengers) are clean, untangled and in good working order.

When attaching a trailer to their vehicle, what must a driver check?
BW0060RU19

That the load is evenly spread.

Proper weight distribution helps to ensure the stability of both the towing vehicle and the trailer. In the trailer, the bulk of the load should be over the axles. If a heavy load is positioned at the front of the trailer, this will result in too much nose weight on the hitch of the towing vehicle and make it difficult to steer. If a heavy load is positioned at the rear of the trailer, this will result in reduced weight on the rear axle of the towing vehicle, which will make it more unstable.

When attaching a trailer to their vehicle, what must a driver check?
That the trailer coupling is attached securely.   BW0061RU19

Before towing a trailer or a caravan, check that the tow bar is securely attached to the towing vehicle, that the trailer coupling is properly attached to the tow bar and locked in place, and that the breakaway cable is properly connected.

What should be done with the airlines of an uncoupled tractor unit?
C0029RU19

They should be stowed away properly.

When uncoupling a tractor unit from a trailer, the air-lines should be stowed safely, using the hooks or other facilities provided for the purpose on the tractor unit. If you dont do this, the lines can get damaged, for example by getting burned by the exhaust system or getting tangled up in the drive shaft.

Why should the fifth wheel drawing plate on an articulated truck be sufficiently greased?
To reduce wear.

C0030R

In order to prevent premature wear on the drawing plate and latching mechanism, the fifth wheel should be cleaned, inspected for damage and re-greased regularly. Keeping the fifth wheel well greased makes it easier to couple and uncouple a trailer, and also allows smoother articulation between the tractor and trailer when turning.

What should a driver check after driving a truck over rough or broken ground?
C0031RU19

That stones are not jammed between the rear twin wheels.

After driving a truck over rough ground, make sure that it has not picked up any rocks or debris between the rear twin wheels. You should also check this as part of your daily routine.

When driving a tipper truck and about to exit a quarry, what should a driver ensure?

C0086RU19

That the tailboard is secured.

Before exiting a quarry, drivers of tipper trucks must ensure that they tailboard has been securely shut. Also make sure that rear lights and reflectors are clean.

When driving a tipper truck and about to exit a quarry, what should a driver ensure?

C4U19

That there are no stones lodged between the twin-wheels.

When driving a tipper truck, the driver must check that there are no stones lodged between the twin wheels. Trapped stones may damage the vehicle's tyres or come loose causing damage or injury to other road users.

When driving a tipper truck and about to exit a quarry, what should a driver ensure?

C5U19

That the diff-lock is disengaged so as to improve road holding.

Before leaving a quarry remember to disengage the diff-lock when returning to normal road surfaces, not doing so can seriously affect handling and stability, cause excessive tyre wear and severe and expensive damage to the differential and axle.

With respect to tyres, what should a driver check for when carrying out a Walk-around Check of the vehicle?

CD1306U19

That they are correctly inflated.

The daily Walk-around Check is an essential first step in an effective preventative maintenance system. Part of the check is to ensure that tyres are correctly inflated.

What should the driver ensure when carrying out an In Cab Check of the vehicle?

CD1308U19

That the horn is working properly.

The daily Walk-around Check is an essential first step in an effective preventative maintenance system. Part of the in-cab portion of the check is to ensure that the horn is working correctly.

With respect to mirrors, what must a driver check for when carrying out an In Cab Check of the vehicle? CD1309U19

That all mirrors are fitted and adjusted correctly.

The daily Walk-around Check is an essential first step in an effective preventative maintenance system. Part of the check is to ensure that all mirrors are fitted and adjusted correctly.

What should the driver check for when carrying out a Walk-around Check of the vehicle in relation to the exhaust? CD1310U19

That it is not loose or excessively noisy.

The daily Walk-around Check in relation to exhausts is to check for any signs of the exhaust being loose or excessively noisy.

With respect to the fuel cap, what must a driver check for when carrying out a Walk-around Check of a vehicle? CD1311U19

That it is properly closed.

The daily Walk-around Check is an essential first step in an effective preventative maintenance system. Part of the check is to ensure that the fuel cap is in good condition and has no leaks.

When carrying out an In Cab Check of the vehicle, the driver should ensure which of the following is working properly? CD1312U19

Demister.

The daily Walk-around Check is an essential first step in an effective preventative maintenance system. Part of the in-cab portion of the check is to ensure that the demister is working correctly.

With respect to the lights, what must a driver check for when carrying out a Walk-around Check of a vehicle? CD1313U19

That they are clean and in good condition.

The daily Walk-around Check is an essential first step in an effective preventative maintenance system. Part of the check is to ensure that the lights are clean and in good condition.

With regard to vehicle checks, which of the following should the driver check after the Walk-around Check and prior to leaving the depot? CD1314U19

Brakes are operating correctly.

Before moving on to a public road, check that there are no air leaks when you press the foot brake.

With regard to vehicle checks, which of the following should the driver check when on-the-road? CD1315U19

The ABS or EBS lights do not remain on.

Once on the road, there are some ongoing checks the driver should make in the first few kilometres. One of these checks is to ensure that the ABS or EBS lights do not remain on after their check sequence is complete, as this may indicate a fault in the system.

With regard to vehicle checks, which of the following should the driver check when on-the-road? CD1316U19

Speed limiter is working correctly.

Once on the road, there are some ongoing checks the driver should make in the first few kilometres. One of these checks is to ensure that the speed limiter is working correctly.

With regard to vehicle checks, which of the following should the driver check when on-the-road? CD1317

Speedometer is operating correctly.

Once on the road, there are some ongoing checks the driver should make in the first few kilometres. One of these checks is to ensure the speedometer is working correctly.

Tyre pressure should be maintained to which of the following specifications for large vehicles? CD1348U19

Per the manufacturer's recommendation.

Tyres must be maintained at the correct pressure. The appropriate pressure differs across different types and models of tyre, so manufacturers recommendations should be followed for the correct pressure required.

What can an increase in the average fuel consumption mean?

CPC1091U19

The vehicle needs servicing.

Having your truck serviced regularly ensures that you get the best performance and best fuel efficiency.

What should the driver check before leaving a bus?

That it is safe to disembark the bus.

D8AU19

When parking a bus, you should make sure that it is in a safe place, the parking brake is on, the engine is switched off, and the electrical master switch is off. Before leaving the cab, check for approaching traffic to make sure it is safe to disembark.

Which of the following is an External Vehicle Check that must be carried out by the driver?

RSA01039

The vehicle access, steps, handholds and surfaces are in good condition.

Access must be clear to avoid falls. All fixed restraints like hand rails are secure with no movement. No raised or sharp protrusions on all types of surfaces.

Which of the following needs to be confirmed before the bus leaves the depot?

RSA01041

ABS/EBS warning lights are working.

All warning lights must operate on a bus before it leaves the depot/garage.

What items should a driver check when carrying out an external walkaround?

RSA01044

Wheel nut pointers are aligned where fitted.

Wheel nut pointers will give early warning on wheel nuts coming loose. It is also essential you visually check that the nuts are not loose.

Safe and Socially Responsible Driving

Alert Driving and Consideration

Why might it be dangerous to drive on a poorly-lit street?
ABMW0262RU19

Pedestrians crossing in a dark area might be difficult to see.

When you are driving along a poorly-lit street, you should take extra care – vulnerable road users such as pedestrians might not be so easy to see. You should always be prepared to react to a change in the traffic situation.

Why might it be dangerous to drive on a poorly-lit street?
ABMW0263R

It may be difficult to make out poorly lit vehicles in the dark areas.

When you are driving along a poorly-lit street, you should take extra care and be prepared to react to hazards such as unlit parked vehicles.

What should a driver do if dazzled by the lights of an oncoming vehicle?

Look to the left-hand edge (nearside) of the roadway and slow down if necessary.
ABMW0266RU19

If you are dazzled by the lights of oncoming traffic, turn your eyes to the left edge (nearside) of the road. If necessary, stop and allow your eyes to recover before driving on.

When should signals (for example, with indicators) be given to other road users?
ABMW0341R

Clearly and in good time to let other road users know your intentions.

Giving signals is a way of telling other road users what you intend to do. So, you should signal properly before moving off, turning right or left, changing lanes, overtaking, slowing down or stopping. Signal clearly and in good time, and keep in mind that giving a signal does not give you the right of way.

What should a driver do when they want to use a mobile phone?
Pull in and stop in a safe place.

BW0001RU19

It is illegal to use or handle a mobile phone while driving. Driving requires all of your attention, all of the time, so you should never use or handle a mobile phone while driving. If you want to use a mobile phone, the only safe thing to do is to find a safe place to stop.

Alighting from or getting on or off the vehicle

Is a driver permitted to pick up or set down a passenger on a motorway?

ABMW0489RU19

A driver is never permitted to pick up or set down passengers on a motorway.

Motorways are designed so that traffic can move faster and more freely. It is illegal and dangerous to stop a vehicle on any part of a motorway except in an emergency or when signalled to do so by a garda.

Before exiting the vehicle on a busy road, what should the driver ensure?

BW0002RU19

Before opening the door the driver should check it is safe to do so.

When exiting from a parked vehicle on a busy road, the driver should check it is safe to do so before opening the door, as there could be cyclists or other traffic passing closely by.

What safety precaution should a driver take when getting out of their vehicle?

BW0115U19

Check all around for approaching traffic and pedestrians before opening the door.

Before opening any door, check for other road users passing, and in particular look out for pedestrians, cyclists and motorcyclists. Exit the vehicle only when it is safe to do so, and close the door as soon as possible. Passengers should exit on the side nearest the kerb wherever possible.

1

2

On a busy road, how should a driver allow passengers out of a vehicle?

Stop and allow them to get out on the side nearest the kerb. BW0116RU19

Before allowing any door to be opened, check for other road users passing, and in particular look out for pedestrians, cyclists and motorcyclists. Passengers should exit on the side nearest the kerb, without getting in the way of pedestrians.

How should a driver exit from the cab of a truck? C0085RU19

Use the steps and handgrips provided while facing towards the cab.

Before exiting the cab of a truck, ensure the parking brake is securely applied, neutral gear is selected and the ignition is switched off, face the cab and use the handgrips and steps provided - do not jump from the cab to the ground.

What should a driver take into account when gaining access to the top of a tanker? C0089RU19

That there may be overhead cables.

If you need to gain access to the top of the tanker, check that the tanker surface is not slippery and that the vehicle is not parked beneath overhead cables. Either of these conditions can cause injury or fatality.

Which of the following sequences of action should a driver follow to safely exit a truck cab? C1312U19

Open door - grab the handgrip - face vehicle - step down backwards.

Before exiting the cab of a truck, ensure the parking brake is securely applied, neutral gear is selected and the ignition is switched off. Open the door, use the handgrips, face the cab and climb down using the steps provided - do not jump from the cab to the ground.

Which of the following driver behaviours help to ensure a safe exit from the trucks cab? C1313U19

Using the proper handgrips.

Open the door, use the handgrips, face the cab and climb down using the steps provided - do not jump from the cab to the ground. However, before exiting the cab of a truck, ensure the parking brake is securely applied, neutral gear is selected and the ignition is switched off.

What should a driver do to secure the vehicle before leaving it? CD0150RU19

Apply the parking brake and switch off the engine.

Before you leave your vehicle, apply the parking brake and switch off the ignition. Check to make sure that you can open the door safely without endangering others, and alight when it is safe to do so.

What precaution should a driver take when allowing passengers to alight from a bus or minibus? CD0152RU19

Make sure that the passengers exit on the side away from the centre of the road.

Before allowing passengers off the bus, a driver should stop close to the kerb on the nearside (leftside) to allow passengers an easy and safe exit from the vehicle.

What precaution should a driver take when allowing passengers to alight from a bus or minibus? CD0152RA

Make sure that the passengers exit on the side away from the centre of the road.

Before allowing passengers off the bus, you should stop close to the kerb on the left to allow passengers an easy and safe exit from the vehicle.

1

2

How should a driver exit the cab of a bus with the driver's door on the offside (right-side)? D0039RU19

By climbing down while facing inwards.

When getting out of the cab of a bus that has the drivers door on the off-side (right-side), the driver should use the grab handles and face inwards, so that they can climb down safely in a gradual manner.

When is it safe to open the passenger door of a bus? D0040RU19

When stopped at a place where it is safe for passengers to get out.

Drivers should only open the door of a bus when it is stopped in a safe place. It is both dangerous and illegal for the passenger door to be opened while a bus is moving.

When children are alighting from a school bus, what advice should a driver give them? D0041RU19

To stay well in off the road until the bus has moved away.

Schoolchildren in particular can be excitable, unruly and unpredictable. When they are getting off the bus, advise them to stay off the road until the bus has moved away and to check that the road is clear before crossing it.

What should a driver do when stopping to allow passengers get off the bus?

D0042RU19

Stop where the passengers getting off the bus will not be in danger from other traffic.

Drivers should only allow passengers to get on and off the bus on the near-side (left side) when it is stopped in a legal, safe and convenient place.

When leaving the cab of a bus, what should a driver ensure?

D0052RU19

That the parking brake is on.

When leaving a bus, drivers should make sure that it is in a safe place, the parking brake is on, the engine is switched off, and the electrical master switch is off.

When leaving the cab of a bus, what should the driver ensure?

D0053RU19

That the electrical master switch is off.

When leaving a bus, drivers should make sure that it is in a safe place, the parking brake is on, the engine is switched off, and the electrical master switch is off.

When letting passengers off a service bus, what should a driver do to ensure their safety?

D1U19

Let the passengers off only when the bus is stopped at a bus stop.

Before opening the doors to let passengers off a service bus make sure that they can alight safely by checking for other road users, such as pedestrians or cyclists, that may be coming up on the near-side (left-side).

When leaving the cab of a bus, what should the driver ensure?

D9U19

That the engine is switched off.

When leaving a bus, drivers should make sure that it is in a safe place, the parking brake is on, the engine is switched off, and the electrical master switch is off.

Anticipation and Reactions

An approaching driver notices that the boy on the children's bicycle has said goodbye to his friend. What is the correct action for the driver to take? ABMW0223RU19

Be prepared for the boy setting off at any moment.

Because it is difficult to predict childrens behaviour, you should always be prepared to react to a change in the traffic situation or to stop.

When approaching the pedestrian crossing, what should the driver do in this situation? ABMW0227R

Slow down in good time and be prepared to stop.

When there are pedestrians at or near a zebra crossing, you should slow down on approach and be prepared to stop to allow the pedestrians to cross safely.

What should the driver do if there are children playing at the edge of the roadway? ABMW0232R

Reduce speed, drive cautiously and remain ready to brake.

Because it is difficult to predict children's behaviour, you should always be prepared to react to a change in the traffic situation and be prepared to stop.

1
2

The silver car is overtaking the parked red car, what should the driver do in this situation?
ABMW0237R

Reduce speed considerably and be ready to stop.

You should read the road and be extra careful while driving through an area where children might be playing. When a ball bounces out on the road you should expect that a child might follow to retrieve the ball.

What should a driver be aware of in this situation?
ABMW0238RU19

The pedestrian may leave the traffic island without paying attention.

You should read the road ahead and expect extra pedestrian activity when the tram is at the stop.

What should the driver be most conscious of in this situation?
ABMW0248RU19

The pedestrian may suddenly cross the road in front of the vehicle.

It is often difficult to predict other road users behaviour. Where there are parked vehicles on both sides of the road you should approach with caution, and be prepared to react to a change in the traffic situation and to stop.

What should the car driver be aware of in this situation?
ABMW0292RU19

Slowing down and being prepared to react.

When you are approaching a bend or corner with a restricted view you should slow down if necessary and be prepared to react to any changes in the traffic situation.

What should a driver be aware of when driving at night along a shopping street with many different light sources? ABMW0294R

Traffic lights may be difficult to distinguish from the other bright lights.

When driving at night in an area where there is a variety of light sources, you need to be extra careful, as potential hazards might be more difficult to see.

What should a driver be most aware of in this situation? ABMW0295RU19

Children may unexpectedly run out from between parked cars.

When driving in a residential area you need to take account of the danger you might pose to children playing. You should always observe warning signs relating to children and drive accordingly.

1
2

What should a driver do in this situation?

Reduce speed and be prepared to stop as other children could follow. ABMW0296R

You should always be aware of other road users especially children, who can be unpredictable and show no road sense. You should drive with extra care in areas where there are children about – for example, near schools, playgrounds and in residential areas.

What should a driver be aware of in this situation?

A dangerous right-hand bend ahead.

ABMW0304R

You should always read the road ahead and be prepared to react to changing traffic situations – in this case paying attention to the warning sign clearly indicating a right-hand bend ahead.

What should the driver do when there is a sharp dip in the road ahead?

Reduce speed, keep to the left and be alert for hazards ahead.   ABMW0314RU19

As you approach a sharp dip in the road, you should be aware that there might be hidden dangers ahead. For example, there might be pedestrians, cyclists or other approaching traffic, or the road could be flooded in the dip. You should always read the road ahead and be prepared to react to changing traffic situations – you might need to reduce your speed and drive with extra care.

What should a driver do if they see a red warning triangle on the road?

The driver should slow down and expect a hazard up ahead.   ABMW0315R

Warning triangles are used to alert approaching traffic that there is a vehicle breakdown or collision ahead. When you come across a warning triangle, you should slow down and be prepared to stop if necessary. Do not allow yourself to be distracted by the incident.

The driver is approaching traffic lights that they know have been green for some time. What should the driver do?   ABMW0316RU19

The driver should be aware that the lights may change before they reach them and be prepared to stop.

You should always read the road ahead and be prepared to react to changing traffic situations. Where traffic lights have been green for some time, you should be prepared to stop, as the lights are probably about to change to amber.

What should a driver do when approaching a junction normally controlled by traffic lights and the traffic lights are not lighting? ABMW0317RU19

Treat it as an unmarked junction and proceed cautiously while watching out for other traffic.

You should always read the road ahead and be prepared to react to changing traffic situations. If the traffic lights are not working, you should approach the junction with extra care, and you should proceed only if it is safe to do so.

What should the driver do if there are cattle on the road ahead?

The driver should reduce speed and pass them with care. ABMW0318RU19

You should always read the road ahead and be prepared to react to changing traffic situations. If you meet cattle or other animals on the road, you should slow down and be prepared to stop . Dont use the horn or do anything that might frighten the animals. You must stop if directed to do so by the person in charge of animals.

What should a driver do if they see horse riders on the road ahead? ABMW0319RU19

The driver should reduce speed, allow extra clearance and pass with care.

You should always read the road ahead and be prepared to react to changing traffic situations. If you meet horses or other animals on the road, you should slow down and be prepared to stop . Dont use the horn or do anything that might frighten the animals. You must stop if directed to do so by the person in charge of animals.

What should drivers be aware of if they meet horses with riders on the road? ABMW0320R

Drivers should be aware that loud noises from their vehicle may frighten the horses and cause them to bolt.

You must know your responsibilities towards animal traffic on the road. Horses are easily startled and any sudden noises or activity could cause them to bolt.

What should the driver do when approaching a humpbacked hill? ABMW0321RU19

The driver should reduce speed, keep to the left and be alert for hazards ahead.

As you approach a humpbacked bridge or hill, you should be aware that there might be hidden dangers ahead – for example, overtaking traffic coming towards you. You should always read the road ahead and be prepared to react to changing traffic situations such as this.

1

2

What danger can arise during daylight when a driver enters an area that is heavily shaded by overhanging trees? ABMW0339RU19
Visibility could suddenly be reduced.

When you enter a heavily shaded area after driving in bright sunlight, it might take a while for your eyes to adjust to the change, and you might not see a hazard immediately ahead.

How does giving a late signal affect other road users? ABMW0343RU19
They may not have been given sufficient time to react.

Giving signals is a way of telling other road users what you intend to do. So, you should signal properly before moving off, turning right or left, changing lanes, overtaking, slowing down or stopping. Signal clearly and in good time, and keep in mind that giving a signal does not give you the right of way. Late signals may confuse other road users.

What should a driver do when approaching traffic lights stuck on red? ABMW0348RU19
Stop and proceed with great caution.

On approach to traffic lights that are stuck on red, a driver should stop and proceed with caution when the way is clear.

What should a driver do when approaching roadworks warning signs?
Reduce speed and be prepared to stop for works vehicles or a ABMW0468RU19
flagman.

A driver should always approach roadworks with caution as there are many possible hazards to deal with – including road workers, works vehicles, uneven road surfaces and temporary traffic controls.

If a driver suspects that their vehicle indicators have not been seen, what should the driver do? ABMW0560RU19
Use a clear, decisive hand signal as well.

If the driver is concerned that for whatever reason the indicators are not giving an adequate signal, they should use clear decisive hand signals as well to advise other road users of their intention.

What should a driver do if they intend to reverse their vehicle into an area which they cannot see?

BW0016RU19

Ask someone to guide you when reversing.

Do not attempt to reverse into an area that you cannot see into properly. You should get assistance from somebody who can guide you safely into the area.

What should a driver do if dazzled by headlights reflecting in the rear-view mirror of their car?

BW0029RU19

Use the night driving mode on their rear-view mirror.

If a driver is being dazzled by the lights of following traffic, they should adjust their rear-view mirror to the night driving mode. This will allow them to concentrate on the road ahead and not be distracted by lights from following traffic.

A driver is driving a long vehicle and wishes to turn left into a narrow side road. What should the driver do?

CD0114R

Be aware that cyclists may come up on the inside if the vehicle has moved to the right to make room to turn left.

If you are driving a long vehicle and wish to turn left into a narrow road, take as much room as you need on the approach to the junction to allow you to complete the turn successfully. This may mean that your vehicle will be to the right of its normal position on the road, and other road users, especially cyclists, may come up on the inside of your vehicle.

When making a turn in an articulated car-transporter, what should a driver be aware of?

CD0122RU19

The front overhang follows a wider line than the cab.

The driver of a car transporter should be aware of the extra height of the vehicle when it is loaded with the cars, the instability of the vehicle when only the top deck is loaded, and, on articulated car transporters, the fact that front overhang does not follow the line of the cab when turning.

| 1 |
| 2 |

Carrying Passengers

How many passengers may be carried on any given bus?

D0023RU19

As many as the vehicle's PSV plate specifies.

The maximum number of passengers that may be carried on a bus is specified on the PSV plate. It is essential that bus drivers familiarise themselves with the maximum capacity as this may have implications for the speed limits that applies to the vehicle.

What is a bus driver's main responsibility?

D0026RU19

The safety and comfort of the passengers.

A bus drivers main responsibility is to ensure the safety and comfort of their passengers. This means delivering them safely to their destination, on time, in a courteous and efficient manner.

What effect could overloading with passengers or luggage have on a bus?

D0028RU19

It can impair the bus's road-holding ability.

Overloading a vehicle can adversely affect its road-holding capabilities . Bus drivers are responsible for the safety and comfort of their passengers, and overloading puts them and the vehicle at risk.

Is it permitted to lock the emergency doors on a bus carrying children?

D0029RU19

No - easy entry and exit from a bus or minibus is essential for safety.

For safety and legal reasons, emergency doors and exits must never be locked when a bus or coach is in service. In the event of a collision or an emergency, occupants egress will be impeded by locked doors.

When driving a double-decker bus, how would a driver monitor the passengers on the top deck?

D0030R

Frequent use of the internal mirrors and cameras if fitted.

Most double-decker buses are fitted with cameras or interior mirrors that are positioned so as to enable the driver to check exits and entrances, stairs and the top deck.

Whilst driving a double-decker bus, what are the interior mirrors used for?
D0031R

Observing passengers who may be standing.

Most double-decker buses are fitted with cameras or interior mirrors that are positioned so as to enable the driver to check exits and entrances, stairs and the top deck.

Whilst driving a double-decker bus, what should the driver use internal mirrors for?
D0031RAU19

To ensure high standards of passenger care and safety.

Most double-decker buses are fitted with cameras or interior mirrors that are positioned so as to enable the driver to check exits and entrances, stairs and the top deck to ensure the safety and comfort of the passengers.

What should a driver do to ensure the safety and comfort of their passengers?
D0032R

Drive smoothly and brake evenly.

If you drive a bus, your main responsibility is to ensure the safety and comfort of your passengers. Read the road ahead and plan well in advance for braking and stopping and for changes in direction. This style of driving will help to ensure that your passengers arrive safely at their destinations.

What driving behaviour could result in passengers getting thrown about?
D0033RA

Cornering harshly.

If you drive a bus, your main responsibility is to ensure the safety and comfort of your passengers. Read the road ahead and plan well in advance for braking and stopping and for changes in direction. This style of driving will help to ensure that you brake smoothly and turn at a speed that does not inconvenience or endanger your passengers.

How can a driver ensure passenger safety?
D0034RU19

By allowing them time to get seated.

A bus drivers main responsibility is to ensure the safety and comfort of their passengers. They should treat passengers with care and respect. When picking up passengers, they must ensure that they are seated before moving off again.

Why should a driver accelerate smoothly?

D0035RU19

To improve passenger comfort.

A bus drivers main responsibility is to ensure the safety and comfort of their passengers. They can do this by reading the road ahead and planning well in advance for any braking, stopping and changes in direction. This style of driving will help to ensure passenger comfort and that they arrive safely at their destinations.

In what circumstances may a driver carry passengers in a trailer attached to a bus?

D0036RU19

It is never permitted.

Passengers must never be carried in the trailer, it is both dangerous and illegal.Bus drivers are responsible for the safety and comfort of their passengers, and for the vehicle itself.

In relation to the vehicles doors, what in particular should a driver be aware of when driving a bus?

That the passenger doors should be locked.

D0043RAU19

For safety and legal reasons, emergency doors must never be locked when a bus or coach is in service. In the event of a collision or an emergency, occupants egress will be impeded by locked doors.

What should a driver be aware of before moving off?

D0059RU19

The effect of any sudden movement of the bus on passengers.

Before moving off, braking, stopping or turning, remember that any sudden movement of the vehicle can cause discomfort or danger to passengers. Those that are standing or moving around the vehicle are particularly at risk.

What should a driver be aware of before moving off from a bus stop?

D12AU19

Persons attempting to board the bus.

Before you close the doors, make sure that all passengers boarding or leaving the bus have done so. Pay particular attention to older passengers who might not be as quick boarding or leaving.

What should a driver be aware of before moving off?
D13AU19

Persons attempting to leave the bus.

Before moving off from a bus stop, drivers should always make sure all passengers boarding and leaving the bus have done so. Pay particular attention to older passengers who might be slow when boarding or leaving.

Which of the following should professional bus drivers do if there are delays on route?
RSA01019U19

Keep passengers informed.

Depending on the type of bus being driven, for bus and coach companies the driver is the public face of the company and represents the company in its dealings with the passengers. Keeping passengers informed will help to reduce frustration and improve a companies image.

From what vehicles first registration date were private buses required to have seat belts fitted?
RSA01020U19

October 2007.

Under Irish law private buses with a first registration date on or after October 2007 must have seatbelts fitted. Drivers should ensure that their vehicles seatbelts are fitted and working, and encourage passengers to them.

What can a bus driver do to avoid harsh braking for the comfort of their passengers?
RSA01022U19

Read the road ahead and plan early.

For the comfort of all passengers, bus drivers should avoid harsh braking by reading the road ahead, this will allow them time to react to the changing traffic situations and if necessary brake early.

1

2

When carrying passengers in darkness why should a bus driver have the interior lights switched on in the vehicle?

RSA01024

In order for passengers to move around the bus safely when parked.

When driving a bus in darkness which has passengers aboard, the interior lights must be switched on, this will allow passengers to move around safely and reduce the chances of a passenger tripping or falling.

What is a legal responsibility of bus driver carrying children?

RSA01026

To ensure that passengers under the age of 17 comply with the requirement to wear a seat belt or child restraint.

Make sure passengers aged under 17 use the correct seat, booster seat, booster cushion or seatbelt. All drivers are legally responsible for this. It is an offence to fail to comply with the above outlined child restraint system requirements. Specifically, it is an offence for a driver to allow a person under 17 years of age to occupy a seat without wearing a seatbelt.

Should a driver issue tickets whilst driving away from the bus stop?

No it can be dangerous and the passenger may fall.

RSA01027

It is dangerous to move a bus whilst passengers are not holding on to handle rails.

Carrying Passengers » Dealing with Customers with Disablities

When dealing with a passenger with a visual impairment a driver should

tell them if there is anything blocking their way as they get on or off the bus.

D1307U19

Alerting a passenger with a visual impairment to the presence of any obstacles in their path helps ensure they get on or off the bus safely.

When dealing with a passenger who is deaf or hard of hearing a driver should

Speak clearly and at normal speed.

D1308U19

Speaking clearly and at normal speed helps a passenger who is lip reading to understand.

When dealing with a passenger with a physical disability D1309U19
give them time to get to their seats before moving off.

Giving a passenger with a physical disability time to get to their seat before moving off
helps to ensure that they have a safe and comfortable journey.

When dealing with a passenger with a learning disability a driver should
be patient and explain more than once if needed. D1310U19

Being patient and explaining more than once if needed helps to ensure that a passenger
with a learning disability understands what you are saying and has a comfortable
experience.

**A wheelchair user boards the vehicle and wishes to use the docking area,
which is occupied with standing passengers and their baggage. What
should the driver do?** D1311
Ask the passengers to move.

A wheelchair user seated in his/her wheelchair must only be carried in a docking area.
Drivers must ensure that the passenger can get in to and out of the docking area and
that it is free for their use.

**To safely deploy a lift or ramp for use by a wheelchair user a driver
should** D1312
Position the vehicle as close as possible to the kerb.

Positioning the vehicle as close as possible to the kerb allows the ramp or lift to be
deployed onto the pavement, helping a wheelchair user to safely and comfortably get on
or off the bus.

**In which of the following locations may a wheelchair user be carried in a
bus or coach?** D1313
In the docking area.

A wheelchair user seated in his/her wheelchair must only be carried in a docking area.

1
2

A dog which is used by a person with a physical, hidden or learning disability is a
D1314U19

assistance dog.

Assistance dogs are trained to undertake practical tasks to support a person with a disability. An assistance dog for a person with a physical, hidden or learning disability acts as a calming focus, enabling a person to remain safe and feel secure in places the person may find challenging.

A driver's responsibility with regard to a wheelchair restraint system is to
D1315U19

ensure that the wheelchair is secured with the appropriate webbing straps or clamps.

To ensure a safe journey, it is of the utmost importance that the wheelchair user is secured in the wheelchair with the appropriate vehicle seatbelt.

What should a driver do before moving off from a stop where the wheelchair ramp was used by a passenger?
RSA01015

Ensure that the wheelchair ramp is safely secured.

Before moving away from a stop where the wheelchair ramp was used, you should always ensure the ramp safely secured in its location for safety reasons.

What should a bus driver do when communicating with a passenger who is hard of hearing?
RSA01023

Driver should look at the passenger when speaking to them.

As a professional bus driver you should be aware of how to communicate with passengers who have special needs. When communicating with a passenger who is hard of hearing you should look at them when speaking to them, this allows for facial expressions to be understood.

What should a driver do when a deaf person gets on the bus?
RSA01028

Look at the passenger when speaking to them.

Drivers must be sympathetic towards passengers who have special needs and treat them fairly.

Driver Behaviour

If involved in a dispute with an angry person who threatens the company with legal action, the driver should   CPC1379U19

remain calm and in control of the situation.

As you represent the company, you must behave in a professional way. The company's reputation and, to some extent, liability depend on you.

When a driver is involved in a dispute while on duty, the company may suffer commercially and financially because   CPC1382

the driver is a representative of the company.

As you represent the company, you must behave in a professional way. The company's reputation and, to some extent, liability depend on you.

Driver Distractions

When driving along and wishing to use a hand-held mobile phone, what should a driver do?   ABMW0380RU19

Stop at a safe location before using the phone.

It is an offence and very unsafe to use a hand-held mobile phone while driving a vehicle or riding a motorbike as it prevents you from concentrating fully on your driving. While using a hands-free phone kit is not illegal, in some circumstances it could be a dangerous distraction, and you could be prosecuted for dangerous driving, careless driving or driving without due care and attention. If a driver needs to make a call they should pull in and stop in a place where it is safe to do so.

A driver using a mobile phone is how many times more likely to have an incident?   CPC1146U19

Four times.

Using a hand-held mobile phone while driving is an offence. It is unsafe because it prevents you from concentrating fully on driving. It is illegal to hold a mobile phone in your hand or to support it on your shoulder.

Driving at Night

When should a driver use dipped headlights?
ABMW0207RU19
From just after dusk to just before dawn.

Lighting up hours are defined as the period of time during which drivers should turn on dipped headlights in order to be seen. This period normally starts half an hour after sunset and ends half an hour before sunrise.

What lights should a vehicle show at dusk?
ABMW0208RU19
Dipped headlights.

Drivers need to see and be seen during all periods of low light levels – for example, at dusk and dawn and in some bad weather conditions. At times of low light, you should turn on dipped headlights. The Road Safety Authority recommends that motorcyclists and drivers turn on their dipped headlights or daytime running lights during daylight hours.

What are the possible consequences of having incorrectly adjusted headlights?
ABMW0439RU19
Oncoming road users could be dazzled.

You are responsible for making sure that your vehicle is roadworthy and that its headlights are adjusted correctly. If the headlights are out of line they are less effective and may dazzle oncoming traffic, even when dipped.

When driving at night and blinded by the lights of an oncoming vehicle, what should a driver do?
ABMW0441RU19
Look towards the verge and slow down and stop if necessary.

If you are dazzled by the lights of an oncoming vehicle, look towards the verge until the vehicle has passed. Slow down and stop if necessary.

A driver has been driving regularly in daylight and must now undertake a journey at night. What should the driver do?
ABMW0442RU19
Drive at a slower speed than in the day as visibility is reduced at night.

If you are not familiar with driving at night time, it can take quite a while to adjust to conditions. For that reason, you might need to drive slower until you get used to the reduced visibility at night.

With regard to vehicle speed, what should a driver do when driving at night?

ABMW0443RU19

Drive at a speed that enables the driver to stop within the distance ahead that they can see to be clear.

When driving at night in good driving conditions the full headlights of a car will typically let you see 100 metres ahead. So, you should travel at a speed that allows you to stop in that distance.

When driving at night, what is the safest approach for a driver to adopt?

Drive at a speed that enables the driver to stop within the distance ahead that they can see to be clear.

ABMW0444RU19

When driving at night in good driving conditions the dipped headlights of a car will typically let you see 30 metres ahead. So, you should travel at a speed that allows you to stop in that distance.

When is it safe for a driver to use the main beam headlights when driving at night?

ABMW0446RU19

When there is no oncoming traffic.

Drivers should use the main beam headlights, to improve visibility, when driving at night in unlit rural areas – this will enable them to see as far ahead as possible. Making sure, however, that these lights are dimmed where necessary to avoid dazzling or inconveniencing other road users.

What lights should a driver have on when driving behind other traffic at night?

Dipped headlights.

ABMW0447RU19

Drivers should dip their headlights when driving behind another vehicle so the driver in front is not dazzled by your lights in their mirror.

When driving at night, when must a driver use dipped headlights?

When meeting or driving behind other traffic.

ABMW0448RU19

When driving at night drivers should dip their main beam headlights when meeting or following traffic to avoid dazzling or endangering other road users.

When dazzled by the lights of an oncoming vehicle, what should a driver do?

ABMW0450RU19

Do not look directly at the lights.

If dazzled by the lights of an oncoming vehicle, do not look directly at the oncoming lights. Instead glance towards the verge until the vehicle has passed and /or slow down and stop if necessary. This will avoid any temporary blindness caused by the brightness of the oncoming lights.

Is a driver allowed to sound the horn while driving in a built-up area at night?

ABMW0721RU19

Yes, but between 11:30pm and 7:00am the horn may be sounded only in an emergency.

Drivers are not allowed to use the horn in a built-up area between 11:30pm and 7:00am unless there is a traffic emergency. Only use a horn to warn other road users of danger or if needed to make them aware of your vehicles presence for safety reasons. Using the horn does not give drivers an automatic right of way. Never use the horn to provoke a reaction from or to rebuke another motorist.

When is the use of the horn prohibited?

ABMW0723RU19

Between 11:30pm and 7:00am in a built-up area.

Drivers are not permitted to sound the horn in a built-up area between 11:30pm and 7:00am unless there is a traffic emergency. Only sound the horn to warn other road users of oncoming danger or if they need to be made aware of your presence for safety reasons. Sounding the horn does not give the driver an automatic right of way. Never sound the horn to provoke a reaction from or to rebuke another motorist.

At night, what effect could driving with a single headlight have on oncoming drivers?

BW0031RU19

They could mistake the vehicle for a motorcycle.

Motor vehicles (except motorcycles) are required by law to have two headlights. A vehicle with only one headlight could be mistaken for a motorcycle and other road users could believe that it is in a different position on the road than it actually is. Vehicle lights should be checked on a regular basis and repair faulty lighting immediately.

When should a driver use the vehicle side lights?
BW0069RU19

When parking on an unlit road.

When leaving a vehicle on an unlit public road at night this creates a potential danger for other road users. Drivers should therefore leave side/parking lights on, so that the vehicle can be seen by other road users. Drivers should not leave headlights on when parked as this may cause other road users to become disoriented.

During normal visibility conditions during daylight which of the following lights does the RSA recommend using?
CD1339

Dipped headlights.

RSA recommends the use of daytime running lights (where fitted) or dipped headlights during daylight conditions.

When driving in a poorly lit area at night, how can a driver avoid dazzling oncoming traffic?
CD1340

Switch to dipped headlights.

When travelling in a poorly lit area at night, dipped headlights help to avoid dazzling an oncoming driver.

A driver is preparing to undertake a journey at night and discovers that dense fog is forecast. How can the driver BEST minimise risk in this situation?
CD1341

Postpone the journey.

If fog becomes thick at night, and a large vehicle is unable to proceed safely, it may become a serious hazard to other traffic. For this reason, if thick fog is forecast at night, it is better not to start out in the first instance.

During what hours is it generally not permitted to sound the horn in built-up areas?
CPC1360U19

7:00 pm and 1:00am.

It is not permitted to use a horn in built-up areas between 11:30pm and 7:00am unless there is a traffic emergency.

Driving Calmly

Why is tailgating (driving too close behind the vehicle in front) dangerous?
ABMW0337RU19
The vehicle will not have sufficient distance to stop safely in an emergency.

If you drive too close to the vehicle in front and it brakes suddenly, you will not have enough time to react. For that reason you should always keep a safe distance from the vehicle in front. One way of calculating a safe distance in dry weather is the two-second rule: allow at least two seconds to elapse between the vehicle in front and your own vehicle passing a fixed point such as a lamp post or sign post.

Is tailgating allowed on a motorway or dual carriageway?
ABMW0338RU19
No, because the vehicle in front may stop suddenly.

If you drive too close to the vehicle in front and it brakes suddenly, you will not have enough time to react. For that reason you should always keep a safe distance from the vehicle in front. One way of calculating a safe distance in dry weather is the two-second rule: allow at least two seconds to elapse between the vehicle in front and your own vehicle passing a fixed point such as a lamp post or sign post.

What should a driver do if another vehicle blocks their right of way at a junction?
ABMW0382RU19
Be patient and show restraint.

You should always try to show restraint. It is important to understand that the right of way is not an absolute right of way, and you must always proceed with caution and with regard for other road users. It's safer and more socially responsible.

A driver who is about to undertake a journey is upset or angry. What should they do?
ABMW0383RU19
A driver should not drive until they are calm.

If you drive when you are angry or upset, you are more likely to be involved in a collision, and more likely to react to other drivers bad behaviour. Take the time to calm down and compose yourself before you set out on a journey.

When being overtaken and there is oncoming traffic, what should a driver do?
ABMW0384RU19

Allow the overtaking vehicle to pass and return safely to the left side of the road.

When you are being overtaken and there are oncoming vehicles, you should show consideration for all the other traffic and allow the overtaking vehicle to move in front of you to avoid the risk of a collision.

When another driver is in a hurry and cuts in front what should a driver do?
ABMW0385RU19

Be patient and not retaliate.

If another driver behaves badly, you should not let it annoy you – show restraint and don't react. Road rage only increases the risk of a collision.

What should a driver be aware of when driving through a section of road where roadworks are ongoing?
ABMW0469RU19

Narrower lanes than usual and restricted shoulder areas.

When travelling through a section of roadworks, a driver needs to be extra careful, as the road surface area may be considerably reduced. It may be narrower, uneven, slippery or there may be loose chippings which may pose a danger for road workers and other road users.

Why is tailgating (driving too close to the vehicle in front) a dangerous practice?
CD1342

It can restrict the driver's view of the road ahead.

If a driver does not have a good view of the road ahead, they may not be able to see or plan for hazards which may occur. Tailgating is dangerous because it restricts the view of the road ahead.

What type of driving can reduce the chance of being in a road incident?
Defensive. CPC1185U19

The RSA advise you to drive your vehicle in a defensive manner, be prepared to stop, sound the horn and brake. Always expect the unexpected.

To whom should a driver report aggressive driving? CPC1348U19
Local Garda Station or Traffic Watch.

Report all aggressive driving incidents to Traffic Watch or a Garda station. They are the best people to deal with aggressive driving.

What is road rage? CPC1350
Uncontrolled anger resulting in intimidation toward another driver.

If you display road rage, it means you have uncontrolled anger that causes you to intimidate or be violent towards another driver.

A driver who is tailgating is CPC1359U19
following the vehicle ahead too closely.

Never drive closer than indicated by the two second rule. If you drive too close to the vehicle in front (tailgating) and it brakes suddenly, you may not have enough time to react.

Driving in adverse weather conditions

After a heavy downpour, why should a driver keep a greater distance from the vehicle in front? ABMW0286RU19

Because wheel-spray may impair visibility.

Heavy rain can affect how well you can see and how well you can be seen by other road users. Because of that you should slow down in heavy rain and keep a greater distance from the vehicle in front.

What should the driver be aware of when crossing road markings such as lines and directional arrows in wet weather? ABMW0326RU19

The required stopping distance is increased due to reduced tyre grip.

You should be aware of the impact of changes in the road surface. For example, road markings and directional arrows can become slippery when wet. Where possible, avoid driving on road markings, and be aware of the increased risk of skidding.

What should a driver do when there are dark clouds and visibility is reduced during daylight hours? ABMW0349RU19

Drive with dipped headlights switched on.

Drivers need to see and be seen during all periods of low light levels – for example, at dusk and dawn and in some bad weather conditions. At times of low light, you should turn on dipped headlights.

What effect does a wet road surface have on a vehicle's braking ability? ABMW0392RU19

Generally, it doubles the braking distance of that required on a dry surface.

When it is wet, your tyres do not grip the road surface as well as when it is dry and your stopping distance is increased. For these reasons you should slow down during or after rain and keep a greater distance from the vehicle in front.

What stopping distance should a driver allow for when driving in snow or icy conditions?

ABMW0397RU19

Up to ten times the normal distance.

When driving in snow or icy conditions a driver should allow a greater distance from the vehicle in front as stopping distances can be increased by up to ten times the normal.

Why does it take longer to stop the vehicle on a wet road?

The tyres have less road grip than in dry weather.

ABMW0399AU19

When driving on wet road surfaces the grip of your tyres is reduced which may lead to significantly longer stopping distances. Drivers should be aware of these conditions and reduce speed as stopping quickly may result in skidding.

What is the effect on the control of the vehicle if there is a film of water between the vehicle's tyres and the road surface?

ABMW0400RU19

Steering and braking will be less effective.

When driving on a road where there is a lot of surface water, a film of water can build up between the tyres and the road surface. When this occurs it is called aquaplaning, it reduces the grip of the tyres on the road and can result in the total loss of control over the vehicles steering and braking.

What should a driver do when driving in slippery road conditions?

Drive at lower speeds and use gentle acceleration and braking.

ABMW0403RU19

When driving in slippery road conditions, drivers should be particularly smooth and gradual in the way they accelerate and brake. This will help to avoid skidding or slipping and helps to maintain control of the vehicle.

What should a driver do when travelling downhill on snow or ice?

Select an appropriate gear and brake gently to control speed.

ABMW0404RU19

When travelling downhill in snow or ice, you should select a lower gear to take advantage of engine braking and use the brakes very gently when you need to.

In wet weather how might a driver judge what is a safe following distance from the vehicle in front?

ABMW0428RU19

By allowing at least four seconds to elapse between the vehicle in front and the driver's own vehicle passing a fixed point.

In wet conditions you should maintain a gap of at least four seconds from the vehicle in front – at least twice as long as in dry conditions.

What lights should a driver use when driving in dense fog?

ABMW0435RU19

Drive with dipped headlights and fog lights.

In dense fog you should use dipped headlights and fog lights (where fitted). Sidelights are not strong enough in fog, and full headlights can reflect off the fog and make it harder to see where you are going.

When should a driver use fog lights on their vehicle?

ABMW0451RU19

Use foglights only in dense fog and falling snow.

A driver should use fog lights only during dense fog or falling snow. They must be switched off at all other times.

When can a driver expect to encounter black ice?

ABMW0452RU19

When the temperature drops close to freezing.

Black ice is an almost invisible and thin coating of ice on the surface of the road. Sometimes it can look like a sheet of water or as if the road is wet.

What should a driver do if there is black ice on the road?

ABMW0453RU19

Avoid harsh braking, steering and acceleration.

If a driver suspects black ice, they should avoid harsh braking, steering and acceleration. This will help reduce the risk of skidding.

1

2

Where is black ice likely to occur on the road?
ABMW0454RU19

In sheltered or shaded areas.

Black ice occurs when moisture freezes on a very cold surface. Exposed roads and bridges can have black ice when other sections of the same road may be clear. Black ice is virtually invisible, and so presents a particular hazard for motorcyclists and drivers. In wintry conditions, if you notice a reduction in tyre noise or if the steering becomes lighter, you should suspect that there may be black ice on the road.

What is the safest practice when driving on icy roads?
ABMW0455RU19

Drive at a slower speed than usual using gentle acceleration and braking.

When driving on icy roads you should avoid harsh braking, steering and acceleration. This will help reduce the risk of skidding.

When driving, what effect could icy roads have on the vehicle?
ABMW0456RU19

The vehicle would be more likely to skid.

Icy roads can have a dramatic effect on the way a vehicle handles, and there can be an increased risk of skidding. When driving on icy roads a driver should avoid harsh braking, steering and acceleration. This will help reduce the risk of skidding.

What should a driver do when driving in slippery road conditions?
Use gentle acceleration and braking.
ABMW0457RU19

Tyres have less grip on the road when it is wet or icy. Slow down in slippery conditions, and keep a greater distance from the vehicle in front.

How should a driver negotiate a steep hill or humpbacked bridge when the road is slippery?
ABMW0458RU19

Drive with extreme caution.

Be extra careful when negotiating steep hills or humpbacked bridges in slippery conditions. Slow down gently on the approach, select the appropriate gear for the speed of the vehicle and use gentle steering and acceleration.

Apart from the risk of skidding, what should the driver be aware of when driving in snow?

ABMW0459RU19

Road signs and road markings may become obscured.

Road signs and road markings may become obscured by snow. If this happens you may have difficulty reading regulatory, warning and information signs. This is the main reason why these signs are different shapes. Drivers should pay particular attention when travelling in these conditions.

What should a driver do when driving in heavy rain?

Be aware that the vehicle may slide or 'aquaplane'.

ABMW0460RU19

On a wet road, a film of water can build up between the tyres and the road surface. This is called aquaplaning and it has the effect of reducing the grip of the tyres on the road, and this affects the steering and braking. For these reasons the driver should slow down during and after rain and keep a greater distance from the vehicle in front.

What is the danger in driving at high speeds on wet roads?

ABMW0461RU19

Danger of 'aquaplaning' or sliding across the road surface.

The driver should moderate their speed during heavy rain or where water is building up on the road surface. This will help to avoid 'aquaplaning' which has the effect of reducing the grip of the tyres on the road, and this affects the steering and braking. For these reasons the driver should slow down during and after rain and keep a greater distance from the vehicle in front.

What should a driver do after passing through a flooded section of road?

Apply the brake pedal lightly at slow speed for a short distance to dry the brakes.

ABMW0465RU19

When driving through a flooded section of road, brakes may become less effective. If this happens, test brakes to ensure that they have not been affected by the water – check mirrors before doing so. If they have been affected, press gently on the brake pedal when driving until they dry out and return to normal.

What should a driver do where a section of road ahead has a shallow flooded area?

ABMW0467RU19

Drive in a low gear as slowly as possible keeping the revs high.

When approaching a stretch of road with shallow flooding, reduce speed and assess the area for any danger. When driving through surface water, drive in a low gear as slowly as possible keeping the revs high to avoid stalling.

After a heavy downpour, why should a driver keep a greater distance from the vehicle in front?

ABMW13U19

Because the required stopping distances is greater.

On a wet road surface, your tyres do not grip the road surface as well as in dry conditions and your required stopping distance is increased. Because of that you should slow down during or after rain and keep a greater distance from the vehicle in front.

If the vehicle's windows are covered with ice, what should the driver do?

Fully clear ice from all windows.

BW0008RU19

Make sure all the windows are completely clear of ice so that the driver can safely observe road and traffic conditions all around. This is especially important when driving in slippery conditions. It is good practice to carry a can of de-icer in the vehicle and if possible to fill the washer reservoir with a de-icing agent.

What should a driver do if the vehicle's windows and mirrors are covered in ice?

BW0009RU19

Switch on the heating system and use a scraper to clear the ice before driving.

Make sure all the windows and mirrors are completely clear of ice so that the driver can safely observe road and traffic conditions all around. This is especially important when driving in slippery conditions. It is good practice to carry a can of de-icer in the vehicle and if possible to fill the washer reservoir with a de-icing agent.

When should rear fog lights be used?
In dense fog or falling snow. BW0026RU19

A driver must only use rear fog lights in dense fog or falling snow. Using fog lights in normal road and weather conditions can dazzle or blind following motorists. Also, fog lights may make brake lights harder to see.

When should rear fog lights be used?
When driving in dense fog or falling snow. BW0027RU19

A driver must only use rear fog lights in dense fog or falling snow. Using fog lights in normal road and weather conditions can dazzle or blind following motorists. Also, fog lights may make brake lights harder to see.

What effect can wet weather have on the vehicle's exterior mirrors?
It can distort the rear vision of the driver. CD0083RU19

When driving in the rain, water droplets can adhere to the exterior mirrors and obscure the driver's view to the side and rear of the vehicle. If the vehicle has heated mirrors, turn them on to clear them. Alternatively, stop periodically to clear them manually.

What is the purpose of having spray suppression equipment fitted to a large vehicle?
CD0086RU19

To reduce the amount of water sprayed up from the wheels.

When a vehicle is driven on a wet road, its tyres throw up spray, and this has the potential to reduce visibility for other drivers. A spray suppression system generally includes mudguards, rain flaps and wheel skirts designed to reduce the amount of spray generated by a vehicle. As part of a daily walk around check a driver should inspect the spray suppression equipment on the vehicle before setting out on a journey, especially in bad weather.

What should a driver do before starting a journey in adverse weather conditions?
CD0099AAU19

Check the weather forecast for the planned route.

Driving in adverse weather conditions is more dangerous and more tiring. Drivers should check the weather forecast and weather warnings and other sources for information on the expected conditions on the intended route, and allow extra time to complete the journey.

What should a driver do before starting a journey in bad weather?

Top up the windscreen washer reservoir.

CD0100RU19

Before starting a long journey in adverse weather the driver should ensure that there is sufficient fluid in the windscreen washer bottle in order to keep the windscreen clear in these conditions.

When driving in heavy rain, what should a driver do?

CD0102RU19

Lower speed to allow for reduced visibility and increased braking distance.

When driving in the rain, your visibility can be severely reduced both by the rain itself and by the spray thrown up by other road users. Stopping distances on wet roads are greater than on dry, and you should reduce speed accordingly.

When driving on a hill, how should a steep descent be negotiated in snow or frosty weather?

CD0103U19

Engage a lower gear early and use gentle braking applications to keep the speed down.

In snow or ice, a vehicle takes longer to stop. Before starting a steep descent in a large vehicle, the driver should reduce speed and select a lower gear, brake gently and only when needed. If the vehicle is fitted with a manually selectable retarder, engage it before starting the descent.

What should a driver do when overtaking a vehicle which is displacing mud and spray?

CD0104R

Use the vehicle windscreen wipers and washer system.

In wet weather, vehicles tend to throw up spray and mud, and this can affect visibility for other road users. Before starting a journey make sure that the windscreen wipers are working and the washer reservoir is topped up. Then use these systems as necessary to clear the windscreen, especially when overtaking other vehicles.

What should a driver do when overtaking a large vehicle that is throwing up spray?
CD0105R

Move out earlier than normal and give extra clearance.

In wet weather, vehicles tend to throw up spray and mud, and this can affect visibility for other road users. To minimize this danger, read the road ahead, and when overtaking move out earlier than usual, giving the vehicle you are overtaking extra clearance. This will reduce the amount of spray being deposited on your windscreen.

What effect can strong winds have on a high-sided vehicle?
CD0106RU19

They can cause the vehicle to blow off course.

When driving a high-sided vehicle in strong winds, the driver should choose a route that avoids high-level roads and bridges, exposed motorways and dual carriageways.

When driving a high-sided vehicle in strong winds, what should a driver avoid?
CD0107R

Suspension bridges.

When driving a high-sided vehicle in strong winds, the driver should choose a route that avoids high-level roads and bridges, exposed motorways and dual carriageways.

What would help to stabilise a high-sided vehicle in windy conditions?
CD0108R

Having a full load.

A high-sided vehicle being driven in strong winds is more stable if it has a full, evenly distributed load.

What effect can strong winds have on a high-sided vehicle?
CD0113R

The winds can reduce the vehicle's stability.

When driving a high-sided vehicle in strong winds, the driver should choose a route that avoids high-level roads and bridges, exposed motorways and dual carriageways.

1

2

What should the driver of a large vehicle be aware of when being overtaken by a motorcyclist in windy weather?

CD0135R

The wind turbulence will make the motorcycle less stable.

When a motorcyclist is overtaking a high-sided vehicle, the turbulence created by the larger vehicle may affect the motorcyclist's stability.

Which of the following can a driver do to control the risk of being dazzled when driving into a low sun?

CD1336

Keep the inside of the windscreen clean.

Drivers can be dazzled when driving into a low sun. The build-up of a film of dirt on the inside of the windscreen can make it even harder to see when driving into a low sun. Keeping the inside of the windscreen clean can help avoid the risk of being dazzled.

Which of the following can a driver do to help make driving in fog safer?

Drive slowly and steadily.

CD1337

Fog is usually patchy and you will pass through areas where visibility varies. Don't be tempted to speed up through the good patches, as you might find yourself suddenly in another dense patch. Driving at a steady, slow speed helps to manage this risk.

When driving in icy or frosty conditions, what braking distance should a driver allow?

CPC1125AU19

Ten times the normal distance.

When driving in Icy and frosty conditions drivers should allow up to ten times the normal braking distance so that the vehicle can be stopped safely when required.

What would a lightness in the steering MOST likely indicate?

CPC1138AU19

Icy surface.

Lightness in steering indicates a loss of traction. This generally happens when the road surface is icy. Ice provides a harder, smoother surface than rain, or snow so it is difficult to avoid skidding and drivers should allow up to 10 times the normal braking distance in order to stop safely.

Driving in Tunnels

In general, which of the following should a driver do before entering a tunnel?
ABMW0515RU19

Ensure that dipped headlights are switched on.

In general , a driver should switch on their dipped headlights before entering a tunnel.

What should a driver do when entering a tunnel?
ABMW0516RU19

Keep a safe distance from the vehicle in front.

The driver should keep a safe distance from the vehicle in front remembering that they are entering a tunnel and tailgating could create an emergency. The minimum recommended safe distance for a car or motor cycle is 50 metres and is 100 metres for all other vehicles. Always remember the 2 second rule.

What should a driver do if there is very heavy traffic congestion in a tunnel?
ABMW0520RU19

Switch on hazard warning lights.

If there is traffic congestion in a tunnel, you should switch on hazard lights and remain patient. Keep a safe distance from the vehicle in front even in slow-moving traffic. Listen for traffic messages on the tunnel radio station, if available.

What should a driver do in the event of a breakdown or incident in a tunnel?
ABMW0524RU19

Switch of the engine and switch on the hazard lights.

If your vehicle breaks down or is involved in a collision in a tunnel, switch on your hazard warning lights, switch off your engine, go to an emergency station and use the emergency phone to alert the tunnel operator.

Before driving through a tunnel, what should a driver do?

CD0153RU19

Check that the height of the vehicle is less than the signed limit.

If your route takes you through a tunnel, you must make sure in advance that your vehicle does not exceed the height limit for the tunnel. Plan your route early because if your vehicle is higher than the limit displayed on the tunnel height-limit sign, you must take an alternative route.

Before driving through a tunnel, what should a driver do?

CD0154RU19

Check the tunnel height before starting the journey.

If your route takes you through a tunnel, you must make sure in advance that your vehicle does not exceed the height limit for the tunnel. Plan your route early because if your vehicle is higher than the limit displayed on the tunnel height-limit sign, you must take an alternative route.

Before driving through a tunnel, what should a driver do?

CD0154RAU19

Check that you have sufficient fuel.

If your route takes you through a tunnel, you must ensure that your vehicle has sufficient fuel to safely pass through.

Before entering a tunnel, what should a driver do in order to improve vision?

CD0156RU19

Take off sunglasses.

Be aware that there is considerably less light available in a tunnel, even with the tunnel lights on. To improve your vision remove your sunglasses before entering the tunnel.

When driving a large vehicle through a tunnel, what should a driver do?

Maintain a safe distance from the vehicle in front.

CD0157RU19

When entering a tunnel in a large vehicle, slow down and allow a 100-metre gap between your vehicle and the vehicle in front. Because of its size, your vehicle might make it more difficult for following traffic to see the road ahead.

When a vehicle is stopped in a tunnel due to congestion what should a driver do?

CD0158RU19

Switch on hazard warning lights.

If, when driving a vehicle through a tunnel, you meet traffic congestion, leave a safe distance between you and the vehicle in front and switch on your hazard warning lights when stationary.

When a vehicle is stopped in a tunnel due to congestion what should a driver do?

CD0159RU19

Switch off the engine.

If, when driving a vehicle through a tunnel, you are halted in stationary traffic for any length of time, you should switch off the engine to reduce fumes in the tunnel and conserve fuel.

What should a driver do if their vehicle is forced to stop in a tunnel due to a breakdown or a crash?

CD0160RU19

Call for help from an emergency station.

If,there is a breakdown or crash in a tunnel, stop, switch off the engine, switch on the hazard warning lights, check the radio for instructions and use the emergency phone at the emergency station to call for help, check all electronic signs in the tunnel for information.

What should a driver do if their vehicle breaks down in a tunnel?

Use the emergency telephone to call for help.

CD0161RU19

If a drivers vehicle stops in a tunnel due to a breakdown, switch off the engine, switch on the hazard warning lights, check the radio for instructions and use the emergency phone at the emergency station to call for help, check all electronic signs in the tunnel for information.

What should a driver do if their vehicle breaks down in a tunnel?

Switch on the hazard warning lights.

CD0162RU19

If a drivers vehicle stops in a tunnel due to a breakdown, switch off the engine, switch on the hazard warning lights, check the radio for instructions and use the emergency phone at the emergency station to call for help, check all electronic signs in the tunnel for information.

If a vehicle being driven through a tunnel goes on fire, what should the driver do?

CD0163RU19

Leave the vehicle immediately and use the emergency phone at the nearest emergency station.

If there is smoke or fire in the vehicle, switch off the engine, leave the vehicle immediately, go to the emergency station and use the emergency phone to alert the tunnel operator and leave the tunnel by the nearest available exit.

1
2

Driving Risk Factors Related to Various Road Conditions

Why must a driver be particularly careful here? ABMW0289R

Because there is an increased danger of skidding.

Where there are fallen leaves on the road surface, your tyres might have reduced grip on the road surface and your braking distances might be greater.

What should a driver do if there is a large oil spill on the road? ABMW0322R

Reduce speed by gently applying the brakes and switch on the hazard warning lights.

Where oil is spilt on the road, your tyres will have reduced grip, and you might be at risk of skidding if you brake sharply. If you do come across oil on the road, brake gently and switch on your hazard warning lights for a short period to alert other traffic to the hazard.

What should a driver be aware of before crossing railway or tram lines?

There may be an uneven surface and tyre grip may be reduced when crossing the rails. ABMW0325RU19

You should be aware of the impact of changes in the road surface. For example, at railway and tram crossings the uneven surface or oil deposits could reduce the grip of your tyres. Slow down as you approach railway or tram crossings and increase your distance from the vehicle in front.

What should a driver do if they encounter loose chippings on a road?
Slow down and allow extra clearance to other traffic. ABMW0401RU19

Where there are loose chippings on the road, you should slow down and comply with any reduced speed limit and leave extra room (or clearance) between your vehicle and other traffic. This will also give you more time to stop if you need to, and it will help to reduce the amount of chippings your vehicle throws up against other vehicles and possible injury to pedestrians.

What effect does patches of oil or diesel have on a road surface?
It reduces the tyre surface grip. ABMW0402RAU19

A patch of oil or diesel on the road can seriously reduce the grip of your tyres on the road and which may result in a possible skid.

A loss of grip between the tyre and the road surface can most likely be caused by
CPC1315U19

harsh acceleration.

1
2

Environmental Matters and ECO Friendly Driving

What should a driver do when they encounter mud on the road?
ABMW0462RU19

Reduce speed and be aware of farm or works vehicles on the road.

Where there is mud on the road you should slow down and be aware that there is a danger of skidding. Your stopping distance will also be greater where there is mud on the road.

What does this dial provide information on?
Engine revolution.
ABMW0662RU19

The rev counter measures the speed of the engine, in revolutions per minute. Generally, the higher the revs, the more fuel the engine is using, so drivers should keep an eye on the rev counter to help drive in a more eco-friendly manner.

What does a rev counter provide information on?
ABMW0663RU19

Engine revolutions.

The rev counter measures the speed of the engine, in revolutions per minute. Generally, the higher the revs, the more fuel the engine is using, so drivers should keep an eye on the rev counter to help drive in a more eco-friendly manner.

What does blue smoke coming from the vehicle's exhaust generally mean?
ABMW0688RU19

The engine is burning oil.

A vehicle can give off blue smoke from the exhaust when it is burning oil. Poor maintenance and worn engines are typical causes. This blue smoke is harmful to the environment and may be costly. Drivers should have the vehicle checked by a competent person.

What is the effect of a worn exhaust?

ABMW0689RU19

The filtering of fumes is reduced and engine noise is louder.

A worn exhaust system can have a number of effects, including increased noise from the engine and more environmentally damaging fumes (as as they are not filtered properly). There are requirements to ensure vehicles are compliant with EU and Irish legislation. Vehicles are tested for compliance during road worthiness testing.

What affect can a faulty exhaust system have?

ABMW0690RU19

It can increase the vehicles noise and pollution levels.

A worn exhaust system can have a number of negative effects, including increased noise from the engine and more environmentally damaging fumes (as they are not filtered properly). There are requirements to ensure vehicles are compliant with EU and Irish legislation. Vehicles are tested for compliance during road worthiness testing.

What is the purpose of a catalytic converter?

ABMW0691U19

It filters exhaust gases and reduces air pollution.

The purpose of a catalytic converter (CAT) is to remove toxic or polluting gases such as carbon monoxide, nitrogen oxide and unburned hydrocarbons from the exhaust emissions. When the CAT is faulty, an engine management warning light illuminates on the dashboard and drivers should seek advice from a competent person.

How does harsh acceleration affect fuel consumption?

ABMW0715U19

Fuel consumption increases.

Harsh acceleration increases fuel consumption.Smooth accelleration helps to reduce fuel consumption and the emissions from vehicles. Try not to over-rev the engine and use the appropriate gear for the speed of the vehicle. When slowing down, take your foot off the accelerator and allow the vehicle to slow progressively before you brake.

What should a driver do to minimise fuel consumption in their vehicle?

Use gentle acceleration and braking.

ABMW0716RU19

Driving smoothly will help reduce fuel consumption. Read the road ahead and adjust speed in good time, and avoid harsh acceleration and late braking.

How does continuous high-speed driving affect fuel consumption?
It increases fuel consumption.   ABMW0717RU19

Driving at continuous high speeds increases your fuel consumption. Vehicles driving at 112km/h consumes approximately 30% more fuel than a vehicle travelling at 80km/h.

What should a driver do to ensure better fuel efficiency from their vehicle?
ABMW0718R

Ensure that the vehicle is regularly serviced.

One of the keys to good fuel efficiency is making sure that your vehicle is well maintained. Servicing should be carried out as recommended by the manufacturer. Checking the tyre pressure regularly can also help ensure good fuel efficiency.

How can fuel efficiency be improved?   ABMW0719RU19
By using gentle acceleration and making gear changes appropriate to speed.

A driver can contribute to their vehicles fuel efficiency by reading the road ahead and driving smoothly. This is achieved by accelerating gently, using the most appropriate gear for the speed they are travelling at and avoiding harsh braking.

What effect does a worn exhaust have on a vehicle?   ABMW0720RU19
It causes noise and gas pollution levels to increase.

A vehicle with a worn exhaust will probably be noisier and will produce more polluting emissions. There are strict regulations governing the noise and emission levels of vehicles, and these are rigorously checked during a vehicles NCT.

In what way do motor vehicles harm the environment?   ABMW0725R
By increasing carbon monoxide levels.

Carbon monoxide is a poisonous gas emitted by vehicle exhausts into the atmosphere. Driving economically and keeping a vehicle well maintained can reduce the level of carbon monoxide emissions.

What can a driver do to maximise fuel efficiency while driving?   ABMW0727RU19
Avoid carrying unnecessary weight.

The more extra weight is in your vehicle, the more fuel you use. Using a roof rack or a roof box increases wind resistance and this also increases fuel consumption – by as much as 15%. Remove roof racks and roof boxes when not in use.

Which action is likely to cause an increase in fuel consumption? ABMW0728RU19
Harsh acceleration.

Harsh acceleration increases fuel consumption. Driving smoothly reduces wear and tear and also improves fuel consumption. Use the highest gear possible without causing the engine to labour.

What alternatives can drivers take to help protect the environment?
Use public transport. ABMW0729RU19

Using public transport helps to protect the environment. Buses, trams and trains are a more environmentally friendly way to move large numbers of people especially in urban areas. Consider using public transport where possible – not only is it more environmentally friendly, but it can also be more cost-effective when you take the cost of fuel and parking charges into account.

What can be achieved by the driving style known as 'Eco-Driving'?
Reduced fuel consumption. ABMW0730R

The advantages of 'eco-driving' include improved road safety, improved fuel consumption and reduced emissions. The eco-conscious driver becomes a more efficient driver because they learn to read the road further ahead and display better anticipation skills. This reduces the need for harsh acceleration and braking which results in a more economical style of driving and a smoother drive.

Which action contributes to Eco-Driving? ABMW0731R
Selecting a high gear as soon as possible.

Eco-driving' contributes to road safety and also reduces fuel consumption and harmful emissions. Eco-conscious drivers will read the road well in advance and avoid harsh acceleration and braking. Fuel consumption can be reduced by using the highest gear possible without causing the engine to labour.

What can be achieved by the driving style known as 'Eco-Driving'?
Improved road safety. ABMW279U19

The advantages of eco-driving include improved road safety, improved fuel consumption and reduced emissions. The eco-conscious driver becomes a more efficient driver because they learn to read the road further ahead and display better anticipation skills. This reduces the need for harsh acceleration and braking which results in a more economical style of driving and a smoother drive.

What can be achieved by the driving style known as 'Eco-Driving'?
Increased fuel efficiency.   ABMW28U19

One of the many advantages of an eco-driving style, includes; increased fuel efficiency, reduced emissions and improved driver safety. The eco-conscious driver becomes a more efficient driver because they learn to read the road further ahead and display better anticipation skills. This reduces the need for harsh acceleration and braking which results in a more economical style of driving and a smoother journey.

Which action contributes to Eco-Driving?   ABMW29U19
Maintaining a steady speed.

One of the many advantages of an maintaining a steady speed, includes; increased fuel efficiency, reduced emissions and improved driver safety. The eco-conscious driver becomes a more efficient driver because they learn to read the road further ahead and display better anticipation skills. This reduces the need for harsh acceleration and braking which results in a more economical style of driving and a smoother journey.

Which action contributes to Eco-Driving?   ABMW30U19
Looking ahead and anticipating.

One of the many advantages of an eco-driving style, includes; increased fuel efficiency, reduced emissions and improved driver safety. The eco-conscious driver becomes a more efficient driver because they learn to read the road further ahead and display better anticipation skills. This reduces the need for harsh acceleration and braking which results in a more economical style of driving and a smoother journey.

What is a possible effect of over-filling the engine with oil?
It could damage the catalytic converter.   BW0083RU19

It is essential that the vehicles engine is not over filled with oil as this can permanently damage the Catalytic converter which is part of most vehicles exhaust systems and removes up to 75% of the carbon monoxide, nitrogen oxide and hydrocarbons from the vehicles exhaust. Damaging this increase exhaust emissions.

When should a lifting axle be used?   C0051RU19
To save fuel when carrying a lighter load.

Rigid lorries, tractor units and trailers are often fitted with lifting axles. These axles may be free running or steered. The advantage of a lifting axle is that it can be raised or lowered to suit the load on the vehicle, thereby saving fuel and tyre wear.

What should a driver do to avoid excessive exhaust pollution from their vehicle?

CD0168RU19

Have the vehicle serviced regularly.

Drivers can reduce the amount of exhaust pollution created by their vehicles by having the vehicle serviced regularly. Drivers can also reduce emissions by using good forward planning, reducing speed, and avoiding severe braking and harsh acceleration.

How would a driver improve efficiency?

CD0169RU19

Use gentle acceleration, braking and smooth gear changes.

To improve fuel efficiency, save money and help the environment, drivers should use gentle acceleration, braking and change gears smoothly, as recommended by the vehicle manufacturer.

How could a driver reduce exhaust pollution?

CD0170R

Make sure that the engine is serviced regularly.

You can reduce the amount of exhaust pollution created by your vehicle by reducing speed, avoiding severe braking and harsh acceleration, and having the vehicle serviced regularly.

To miss out on a gear while changing down through the gearbox can result in

CPC1058U19

lower fuel consumption.

When a driver doesn't go through every gear while changing down, the engine revs less and uses less fuel.

How can a driver save fuel by using gears?

CPC1060U19

By engaging one that does not make the engine struggle

By engaging a high gear that does not make the engine struggle, fuel efficiency can be achieved.

Which gear should be used to optimise fuel consumption?

CPC1067U19

The highest gear possible without making the engine struggle

By engaging a high gear that does not make the engine struggle, fuel efficiency can be achieved.

1
2

What technique should be used when moving off?

CPC1068U19

Pull away smoothly.

A driver should drive away smoothly for maximum safety and fuel efficiency.

To improve fuel economy, a driver should change down to the appropriate gear, but

change gears when speed has decreased.

CPC1072

When changing down you should wait until your vehicle speed decreases so as not to over-rev the engine, which would use more fuel and cause engine wear.

For the most efficient use of power and fuel, the driver of a vehicle with a full load should

CPC1079U19

use the accelerator smoothly and progressively.

Rapid acceleration and over-revving the engine uses more fuel and causes wear on the engine. When starting off, regardless of load, you should accelerate smoothly.

What effect do heavy braking and rapid acceleration have on fuel consumption?

CPC1081U19

Heavy braking and rapid acceleration increase fuel consumption.

For greater fuel efficiency, speed up gradually, slow down gradually, and drive smoothly in as high a gear as possible.

Compared to one with a petrol engine, a vehicle with a diesel engine can pull more weight at a

CPC1391

lower engine rpm.

Diesel engines give maximum power at minimal fuel consumption because they are high compression-ignition engines. The higher compression uses less fuel for ignition.

To save fuel, the driver should

CPC1402U19

drive smoothly in as high a gear as possible

Driving in a higher gear uses less fuel.

Fitness to Drive / Drug and Alcohol

What effect does alcohol have on driver behaviour?
It slows down a driver's reactions.   ABMW0388RU19

Alcohol is a major factor in collisions that can lead to death and injury. Even small amounts of alcohol affect your judgement and ability to drive.

What effect does drinking alcohol have on a driver?   ABMW0389RU19
It reduces concentration.

Alcohol is a major factor in collisions that lead to death and injury. Even small amounts of alcohol affect your judgement, your concentration and your ability to react to hazards. A driver should never ever drink and drive.

If a motorist or a motorcyclist is taking medication which may affect their driving, what should they do?   ABMW0390RU19
Seek medical advice in relation to driving.

Some medication can affect a drivers ability to drive safely. If you are on medication of any kind, you should ask your doctor or pharmacist to tell you if it is safe to drive while taking it. Read the patient information leaflet supplied with the medication.

For how long may some drugs remain in the body?   CPC1278U19
Up to 72 hours.

Unlike alcohol, the effects of which last for about 24-48 hours, many of the effects of drugs will remain in the body for up to 72 hours.

It is an offence for a professional driver of a bus or truck to drive such a vehicle when that driver's blood alcohol level is above   CPC1279AU19
20 mg per 100 ml.

All drivers are effected by drinking even small amounts of alcohol. Alcohol effects judgement, vision, coordination and reaction time.

What are the drink driving penalties for a learner driver with a blood alcohol concentrate (BAC) of 20mg to 80mg per 100 millilitres of blood?
€200 fine and 3 months driving disqualification.
RSA0200

Alcohol is a major factor in crashes that lead to death and injury. Research proves that even small amounts of alcohol affect your judgement and ability to drive. It is illegal to drive with alcohol levels above the legal limits.

What are the drink driving penalties for a professional driver holding a full car licence and found to have a blood alcohol concentrate (BAC) of 20mg to 80mg per 100 millilitres of blood?
RSA0201
€200 fine and 3 months driving disqualification.

Alcohol is a major factor in crashes that lead to death and injury. Research proves that even small amounts of alcohol affect your judgement and ability to drive. It is illegal to drive with alcohol levels above the legal limits.

What are the drink driving penalties for a driver with a blood alcohol concentrate (BAC) of 80mg to 100 mg per 100 millilitres of blood?
€400 fine and 6 months driving disqualification.
RSA0202

Alcohol is a major factor in crashes that lead to death and injury. Research proves that even small amounts of alcohol affect your judgement and ability to drive. It is illegal to drive with alcohol levels above the legal limits.

What is the penalty for a driver who refuses to give breath, blood or urine samples as evidence for a second offence to An Gárda Síochána?
Automatic disqualification for 6 years.
RSA0203

Alcohol is a major factor in crashes that lead to death and injury. Research proves that even small amounts of alcohol or drugs affect your judgement and ability to drive. It is illegal to drive with alcohol levels above the legal limits, or while under the influence of drugs. It is an offence to refuse to give a breath, blood or urine sample.

Can An Gárda Síochana conduct roadside testing for drugs and alcohol in the mornings?
Yes, they can check at any time.

RSA0204

It is against the law to drive a car, motor bike, truck, bus, pedal bike or an animal-drawn vehicle while 'under the influence of an intoxicant to such an extent as to be incapable of having control of the vehicle'. Intoxicants include alcohol and drugs, whether taken separately or together. The word 'drugs' here includes legal prescribed and over-the-counter (OTC) medicines.

Along with an impairment test, what may a Gárda request if they suspect a driver of driving under the influence of drugs?
A saliva sample.

RSA0205

If a driver is stopped at a roadside check, they should be aware that, along with the impairment test, Gardaí can also request a saliva sample if they suspect the driver is driving under the influence of drugs.

1
2

What is the maximum penalty on conviction for drug driving?
€5,000 fine and 6 months in prison.

RSA0206

Drivers should be aware of the severe penalties if they chose to drive having taken drugs and are detected. Drug driving is extremely dangerous due to the effect drugs have on the brain.

Do the limits for drink and drug driving differ if detected in the morning?
No, they are the same at all times.

RSA0207

The limits for drink and drug driving do not change depending on the time of the day drivers are checked. Drink and drugs remain in the body for a period of time. A driver should think carefully before driving a vehicle the morning after taking drink or drugs, and be aware that they could still be well over the limit.

Fitness to Drive / Drug and Alcohol »
Fatigue

When driving late at night what should a driver be aware of? ABMW0449RU19
That there is a danger of themselves or other drivers falling asleep.

Driving when tired can be very dangerous and driver fatigue is one of the main causes of serious road collisions. If a driver becomes drowsy while driving, they should stop in a safe place take a caffeine-based drink and take a short nap. After this they should then get some fresh air and stretch their legs for a few minutes before setting off again. The only cure for fatigue is proper sleep. Never ever drive when tired.

What should a driver do in order to keep alert during a long journey?
Increase the air circulation and stop if necessary. BW0018RU19

While on a long journey, a driver should take regular rest breaks. A short walk and a caffeinated drink (tea or coffee) can help to revive them. The vehicle should be kept cool and well ventilated with a steady flow of fresh air.

What can a driver do to stay alert on a long journey? CD0032U19
Stop, park in a safe place and have a cup of coffee.

If a driver continues to drive fighting sleep it can be the same as being over the drink driving limit. Stopping the vehicle in a safe place, drinking caffeine and taking a nap for 15 minutes will revive the driver allowing them to continue for a short period.

What can make a driver feel sleepy? CPC0232
Eating a large meal.

Don't drive after a heavy meal as it may make you sleepy.

After driving for a number of hours and feeling sleepy, what is the best action a driver can take to avoid an incident?
CPC1172U19

Stop and drink a cup or two of strong coffee or a caffeinated drink and take a nap for a maximum of 20 minutes.

You should stop and drink a cup or two of strong coffee or a caffeinated drink and take a nap for a maximum of 20 minutes. Caffeine takes about 20 minutes to take effect. If you nap for more than 20 minutes you might wake feeling groggy.

What could badly affect a driver's reactions, especially in an emergency?
CPC1231U19

Feeling tired.

You should not drive while tired or fatigued. Research has shown that tired drivers are a major road safety risk both to themselves and to others.

What type of food does the body digest slowly so one doesn't feel hungry?
CPC1262U19

Pasta.

Slowly digested calories such as pasta, bread, rice and vegetables will keep you satisfied and prevent hunger than those high in sugar.

What type of food does the body digest slowly so one doesn't feel hungry?
CPC1265U19

Bread.

Slowly digested calories such as pasta, bread, rice and vegetables will keep you satisfied and prevent hunger than those high in sugar.

In case of delays, what is the best drink to carry on a journey?
CPC1266U19

Water.

Water is the ideal drink. It quenches thirst longer than drinks such as tea and coffee.

What food is high in protein?
CPC1268U19

Fish.

Meals based on protein containing foods such as fish, meat, eggs, cheese and peas or beans will keep you satisfied and prevent hunger for longer than those high in sugar.

What drink quenches thirst for longer than any other?
CPC1269U19

Water.

Water is the ideal drink. It quenches thirst longer than drinks such as tea and coffee.

What food is high in protein?
CPC1271U19

Eggs.

Meals based on protein containing foods such as fish, meat, eggs, cheese and peas or beans will keep you satisfied and prevent hunger for longer than those high in sugar.

What is the advice given to a driver when feeling tired or fatigued?

You should not drive.
CPC1284U19

Which of these is a symptom of tiredness?
CPC1455U19

Poor physical coordination

When you are tired you are much less alert, have poor physical coordination, and your reaction times are much slower.

What may cause a driver to feel tired when driving?
CPC1456U19

When driving on main roads with low traffic volumes

You are more likely to become tired when driving on main roads, with low traffic volumes (particularly on motorways), where the driving task is relatively monotonous and there is very little stimulation

Journey Planning

What is the maximum permitted distance between a drawing vehicle and a trailer?
C0081R

4.5 metres.

The maximum permitted distance between a drawing vehicle and a trailer is 4.5 metres. A larger distance between the vehicles might lead other road users to believe that the two vehicles were independent and they might try to enter the space between them.

When estimating the time for a journey, what should a driver allow extra time for?
CD2

Stoppages due to road works.

A journey will nearly always take longer than expected because of traffic jams, road works, adverse weather conditions, and so on. A driver should understand this and allow sufficient time to complete the journey in a safe manner.

When estimating the time for a journey, what should a driver allow extra time for?
CD3

Driving during adverse weather conditions.

A journey will nearly always take longer than expected because of traffic jams, road works, adverse weather conditions, and so on. A driver should understand this and allow sufficient time to complete the journey in a safe manner.

When estimating the time for a journey, what should a driver allow extra time for?
CD5U19

Delays due to traffic congestion.

A journey will nearly always take longer than expected because of traffic jams, road works, adverse weather conditions, and so on. A driver should understand this and allow sufficient time to complete the journey in a safe manner.

Managing Speed

Subject to the speed limit, what is the 'safest' speed to drive at?
The speed that will enable the driver to stop the vehicle within the distance ahead that they can see to be clear. ABMW0379U19

You should always drive at a speed that allows you to stop within the distance that you can see to be clear ahead. If you dont think you could safely bring the vehicle to a stop within the range of what you can see, then you're driving too fast – slow down.

What is the recommended minimum stopping distance for a car travelling at 50Km/h on a dry road? ABMW0406RAU19
25 metres.

The total minimum stopping distance of a vehicle depends on four things; perception time, reaction time, the vehicles reaction time and the vehicle braking capability. The recommend minimum stopping distance of a car driving at 50km/h under dry conditions is 25 metres.

What is the recommended minimum stopping distance for a car travelling at 50km/h on a wet road? ABMW0407RAU19
36 metres.

The total minimum stopping distance of a vehicle depends on four things; perception time, reaction time, the vehicles reaction time and the vehicle braking capability. The recommend minimum stopping distance of a car driving at 50km/h under wet conditions is 36 metres.

What is the recommended minimum stopping distance for a car travelling at 100km/h on a dry road? ABMW0408RAU19
70 metres.

The total minimum stopping distance of a vehicle depends on four things; perception time, reaction time, the vehicles reaction time and the vehicle braking capability. The recommend minimum stopping distance of a car driving at 100km/h under dry conditions is 70 metres.

What is meant by the term jack-knifing?

BW0066RU19

When the trailer is travelling faster than the drawing vehicle.

Towing a trailer or caravan dramatically reduces the stability of the towing vehicle. If a driver brakes sharply or slows down quickly, the trailer may pivot around the tow hitch coupling, causing both vehicles to go off course, and possibly overturn.

What does a speed limiter do?

CD0058R

Prevents the vehicle from exceeding a pre-set speed.

A speed limiter is a device fitted to HGVs and buses which sets the maximum speed at which the vehicle can travel.

When driving an unfamiliar vehicle what should a driver do?

CD0110RU19

Drive initially with extra care and at a lower speed than normal.

If you are required to drive a vehicle that is different to the vehicle you normally drive or with which you are unfamiliar, you should take time to familiarise yourself with the controls and operating systems. When driving the vehicle initially you should take extra care and drive at lower speeds than usual until you become accustomed to the vehicle.

How can a driver reduce speed without using the footbrake?

CD9

By lifting their foot off the accelerator.

If a driver reads the road ahead and reacts early enough, they can generally (unless going downhill) reduce speed simply by taking their foot off the accelerator. This style of driving prolongs the life of the vehicle's brakes, reduces fuel consumption and emissions, and improves passenger comfort.

In the interests of safety, what should a driver do when approaching a sharp bend?

CPC1078U19

Change down gears.

If necessary, change down gears as you approach a sharp bend on the road.

How do road speed limiters work?
CPC1397U19

By reducing fuel to the engine

Road speed limiters receive a road speed signal from a sensor or the tachograph. They use that signal to reduce the amount of fuel to the engine.

Multi Lane Driving

What should a driver do when joining a motorway from a slip road?
Try to match the vehicle speed to that of traffic already on the motorway and merge into it in a suitable gap.
ABMW0488RU19

When joining a motorway a driver should try to match their speed to that of the motorway traffic and merge into it when a suitable gap appears, avoiding driving in the hard shoulder, while yielding to traffic already on the motorway.

When driving on a motorway, what should a driver do if they miss their exit?
ABMW0490RU19

Leave the motorway at the next exit and cross to the other side using the fly-over (or underpass).

If a driver misses their intended exit when driving on a motorway, they should proceed to the next junction exit where they can leave the motorway and then rejoin it on the opposite side of the motorway.

What should a driver do when entering a slip road after leaving a motorway?
ABMW0492RU19

Comply with the speed limit on the road the driver is joining.

When a driver is leaving a motorway, they should enter the deceleration lane and reduce their speed. They should comply with the speed limit of the road they are entering.

What should a driver do if they drive past their intended exit by mistake?
Drive on and leave at the next exit.
ABMW0493RU19

If a driver misses their intended exit when driving on a motorway, they should proceed to the next junction exit where they can leave the motorway and then rejoin it in the opposite direction.

What is the main difference between driving on a motorway and driving on other types of road?

ABMW0494RU19

Traffic is generally permitted to travel at a higher speed on a motorway.

Motorways are designed so that traffic can move faster and more freely, without traffic lights, crossroads, level crossings and other road features that might slow down traffic. There are also restrictions on who may use a motorway – for example L-drivers and motorcycles under 50cc are prohibited.

On a 2-lane motorway, what procedure should a driver adopt when wishing to overtake another vehicle safely?

ABMW0495RU19

Use their mirrors, signal and overtake in the right-hand lane when it is safe to do so.

When a driver wants to overtake on a motorway, they should generally only overtake on the right unless traffic is travelling in slow moving queues. The driver should use the Mirror–Signal–Mirror (blind spots)–Manoeuvre routine. Check mirrors, signal intention, check mirrors again (and blind spots), and complete the manoeuvre when it is safe to do so. They should pay particular attention to the speed of the traffic behind them before they move out. When they have finished overtaking, they should move back into the left-hand lane smoothly.

1

2

When joining a motorway from a slip road, what should a driver do?

Adjust speed to match that of the motorway traffic , and merge into a suitable gap.

CD0173RU19

When joining a motorway from a slip road drivers should adjust their speed to that of the motorway traffic on the acceleration lane and merge into a suitable gap in Lane 1. Do not force other traffic to swerve or slow down to avoid your vehicle.

A large vehicle is being driven up a steep hill where the nearside (left hand) lane is marked 'slow lane'. What should the driver do?

CD0174RU19

Drive in the slow lane to allow other traffic to overtake.

Slow lanes (sometimes referred to as crawler or climbing lanes) have been introduced on some roads to allow large slow-moving vehicles to keep in allowing faster-moving traffic to pass more safely. When driving a large vehicle, you should use such lanes where possible to help improve traffic flow.

What is the MOST likely cause of multiple pile-ups on motorways?
Driving too close. CPC1139U19

You should always be able to stop within a distance you can see to be clear. You need to be able to control the vehicle you are driving to the extent that you can stop without causing a problem for anyone else on the roadway. The rule means you must be alert and exercise due care and attention at all times.

Observation and Mirrors

What is the correct action to take in this situation? ABMW0222RU19
Keep a close eye on the children and be prepared to brake in good time.

Because it is difficult to predict childrens behaviour, you should always be prepared to react to a change in the traffic situation or to stop.

What should the driver do when approaching this situation? ABMW0249RU19
Reduce speed and remain ready to brake since the girl on the footpath could suddenly cross the road.

It is often difficult to predict other road users behaviour. You should be prepared in case the pedestrian steps onto the road and the silver car stops suddenly.

What might be described as a bus driver's 'blind spots'? ABMW0352RU19
The areas to the front, sides and rear of the bus which the driver cannot see.

A blind spot is an area that a driver cannot see when looking forward or when looking in the mirrors. The bigger the vehicle, the bigger the blind spots, and you should keep this in mind if you are driving behind a bus. If you are driving behind a bus and you cannot see the bus mirror, then the bus driver cannot see you.

Where are the blind spots on a truck (for its driver) that a driver in a car behind the truck needs to be aware of?
ABMW0353RU19

The areas to the front, sides and rear which the driver of the truck cannot see.

A blind spot is an area that a driver cannot see when looking forward or when looking in the mirrors. The bigger the vehicle, the bigger the blind spots, and you should keep this in mind if you are driving behind a truck. If you are driving behind a truck and you cannot see the trucks mirror, then the truck driver cannot see you.

Where are the blind spots that a driver needs to be aware of when towing a loaded trailer?
ABMW0354RU19

The area to the side and rear of the vehicle and the trailer that the driver cannot see.

A blind spot is an area that a driver cannot see when looking forward or when looking in the mirrors. You should check your blindspots before changing direction or changing lane. The bigger the vehicle, the bigger the blind spots, and you should keep this in mind if you are driving behind a large vehicle, such as one towing a loaded trailer. In this situation, if you cannot see the towing vehicles mirror, then the driver of that vehicle cannot see you.

1
2

What should a driver who wishes to perform a U-turn do?
ABMW0357RU19

Check that the road is not one way.

If you want to do a U-turn you must first choose a place where it is safe and legal to do it. Check all around for other road users and do not impede their right of way. Complete the manoeuvre efficiently and safely.

What should a driver do when they want to safely change to the lane on the right in which there is other traffic?
ABMW0387RU19

Use the mirror, signal and move into the right-hand lane when a suitable gap appears in the traffic in that lane.

Any time you change lanes, you should use the Mirror–Signal–Mirror (blind spots)–Manoeuvre routine. Check your mirrors, signal your intention, check your mirrors again (and your blind spots), and when a suitable gap becomes available manoeuvre the vehicle into the next lane, giving way to traffic already in that lane.

What should the driver be able to see in the vehicle mirrors when they are properly adjusted?
ABMW0683RU19

The area behind and to each side of the vehicle.

Properly adjusted vehicle mirrors enable drivers to see the road behind and to the sides. This helps drivers to take into account what's happening behind them, so that they can make informed, correct and safer decisions.

What should the driver be able to see in the exterior mirrors of a vehicle when they are properly adjusted?
ABMW0684RU19

The area to each side of the vehicle.

Exterior mirrors enable drivers to see the area on each side of the vehicle. Drivers must take into account all visible hazards in order to make informed, correct and safer decisions.

The vehicle's exterior mirrors are covered by a film of mud and dust. What should the driver do?
ABMW0685U19

Clean them with a cloth or tissue before starting their journey.

The purpose of mirrors is to increase the drivers view to the rear and sides of the vehicle and to enable them to take into account all visible hazards. Proper use will enable drivers to make informed, correct and safer decisions. Drivers should ensure that all mirrors, including the exterior ones, are clean and properly adjusted at all times to ensure optimum view.

What effect can wet weather have on a vehicle's exterior mirrors?
Water droplets can obscure the reflected image.
ABMW0687U19

When driving in wet weather conditions, small water droplets can form on the glass of the exterior mirrors. This could make it more difficult to see the road behind and to the sides. Switch on the mirror demisters, if they are fitted. If necessary, stop and clear them.

When towing a high and wide-bodied trailer what should a driver do?
Make use of extended mirrors to check for following traffic.
BW0006RU19

When towing a high and wide-bodied trailer, a driver should use extended mirrors on both sides of the towing vehicle. This will allow the driver to better observe the traffic situation behind and to the sides.

What specific observations should a driver make before reversing their vehicle?

BW0012RU19

Look over both shoulders and behind.

Before reversing, look over both shoulders and to the rear to check all around that there are no children or other road users around the vehicle and that it is safe to reverse.

What specific observations should a driver make before reversing a vehicle fitted with an external audible warning device?

BW0013U19

Observations should be made to the front, sides and rear of the vehicle, including blind spots.

Drivers should not rely solely on an external audible warning device to warn others that their vehicle is reversing. Before reversing, drivers must make sure it is safe to do so by taking all appropriate observations to the front, sides and rear of the vehicle, including the blind spots. Never assume it is safe to reverse just because the vehicle has an external audible warning device.

What should a driver do when they intend to reverse into a side road?

Check carefully all around before and during the reverse.

BW0014RU19

Before and while reversing into a side road, check all around to make sure it is safe and clear to carry out the manoeuvre, paying particular attention to pedestrians crossing behind the vehicle and any other road users.

What should a driver check before reversing into a loading bay?

C0072RA

For the presence of other people.

When reversing in haulage and distribution yards, you must watch out for people getting in and out of adjacent vehicles and pedestrians who may walk behind the vehicle.

When driving a large vehicle, what is the most effective way for the driver to ensure that they can see to the side and rear of the vehicle?

Making full use of all of the exterior mirrors.

CD0141RU19

When driving a large vehicle a driver should make full use all of their exterior mirrors so that they are constantly aware of what is happening around them, and that they can react and respond appropriately.

When preparing to perform a manoeuvre, drivers should follow which of the following activity sequences? CD1318U19

Mirror - Signal - Mirror and check blind spots - Manoeuvre.

Drivers must always use the mirrors effectively before any manoeuvre. The Mirror Check-Signal-Manoeuvre routine ensures that they look before they signal, signal before they act and act sensibly based on what they see in the mirrors.

Drivers should check their nearside mirror every time they pass CD1319

a parked vehicle.

Drivers should always have a good idea of what's happening to the rear, as well as in-front, of the vehicle when performing a manoeuvre such as passing a parked vehicle.

When preparing to perform a manoeuvre, mirrors must FIRST be used
before the manoeuvre. CD1320

Drivers must always use their mirrors effectively before any manoeuvre.

Which of the following driver behaviours is considered the most effective use of mirrors? CD1322U19

Acting sensibly as a result of what is seen in the mirrors.

Effective use of mirrors requires more than simply looking in the mirrors. It requires acting sensibly based on the information observed in the mirrors.

A driver sees a parked car some distance ahead. Preparing to move out, the driver checks the offside mirror. The primary reason for this mirror use is to CD1325U19

check for a vehicle that may attempt to overtake from the rear.

The primary danger when moving out to pass a parked car is that someone may attempt to overtake you as you need to move out. Checking the offside mirror enables the driver to identify this risk.

What is the rule relating to the "safe headway" (a safe distance between two vehicles on the road) when weather conditions are good? CPC1346U19
The two second rule

In traffic, the distance between your vehicle and the one in front of you is known as the safe headway. Keep a safe headway by ensuring that you are at least 2 seconds behind the vehicle in front. This is known as the two second rule.

Having dropped off passengers, what should a driver check before moving off? D0027RU19
Both exterior mirrors.

Before moving off, check your off-side (right-side) exterior mirror for overtaking traffic and other road users and your nearside (left-side) exterior mirror for intending passengers rushing to catch the bus. Check these mirrors as many times as necessary to ensure it is safe to move off.

1

2

Overtaking and Passing

When may you pass another vehicle on the left-hand side? ABMW0212RU19
When the vehicle in front is signalling to turn right or in slow moving lanes of traffic.

Normally you must overtake on the right. There are, however, circumstances where you may overtake on the left – for example, when the vehicle has moved out and signalled to turn right.

What should a driver do when overtaking parked vehicles in a residential area? ABMW0396RU19
Allow sufficient clearance when passing.

When you are passing parked vehicles in a residential area, move into a safe overtaking position in good time and leave plenty of clearance between your vehicle and the parked vehicles to increase visibility of small children in the area and in case someone opens their car door in front of you.

What should the driver of a large vehicle consider before overtaking another large vehicle?
CD0136RU19

The speed of the vehicle being overtaken.

Before overtaking another large vehicle, the driver of a large vehicle needs to assess the road ahead, and take into consideration the speed of the vehicle they are driving and the speed of the vehicle they intend overtaking. They should be sure that they can complete the manoeuvre safely. Overtaking a large vehicle with a large vehicle takes more time and greater distance than a similar manoeuvre involving two cars.

What should the driver of a large vehicle consider before overtaking another large vehicle?
CD0137RU19

The width and condition of the road.

Before overtaking another large vehicle, the driver of a large vehicle needs to assess the road ahead, and take into consideration the size and speed of the vehicle they are driving and the size and speed of the vehicle they intend overtaking. They should be sure that they can complete the manoeuvre safely. Extra clearance is needed to overtake wider vehicles safely. If the road is uneven, the stability of the vehicle can be affected. The driver may need to wait for a safer place to overtake.

After overtaking another large vehicle, what should a driver do before moving back into the left-hand lane?
CD0138RU19

Check the left-hand mirror, signal, and move back when it is safe to do so.

Before overtaking a large vehicle on a dual carriageway or motorway, you should check your right-hand mirror, signal and move out into the right-hand lane when it is safe to do so. After overtaking the vehicle, check your left-hand mirror, signal and move back in to the left-hand lane when it is safe to do so. Do not cut too quickly across the vehicle you have just passed.

In which of the following situations is overtaking on the left permitted?
CD1326U19

The overtaking driver has signalled that they intend to turn left.

Drivers must normally overtake on the right. However, overtaking on the left is allowed in some situations, including when the driver has signalled that they intend to turn left.

When going straight ahead at a roundabout, what should a driver give way to?
CD1327U19

Traffic coming from the right only.

At the majority of roundabouts, for safety and to maintain the flow of traffic, approaching traffic is required to give way to traffic coming from the right.

Roundabouts

When approaching a roundabout, to whom should a driver give way? ABMW0507RU19

The driver must give way to traffic approaching from the right or already on the roundabout.

Drivers should always approach roundabouts with caution. They should be prepared to give way to traffic on the right, traffic already on the roundabout, pedestrians already crossing and to always stop if necessary.

In general, where two lanes are provided on the approach to a roundabout, which lane should a driver select when they intend taking an exit to the right (past the 12 o'clock position) of the roundabout?

The right-hand lane. ABMW0509RU19

When a driver approaches a roundabout where two lanes are provided, they should choose the most suitable one based on the road markings and the exit they intend to take off the roundabout. The left lane is generally used for vehicles exiting to the left (9 o'clock) or straight ahead (12 o'clock) and the right is for vehicles exiting at any exit after 12 o'clock.

What position should a driver generally adopt on approach to a roundabout when intending to take the first exit to the left? ABMW0510RU19

Approach in the left-hand lane.

When a driver intends to take any exit between the 6 O'Clock and 12 O' Clock positions they should generally approach the roundabout in the left lane unless road markings dictate otherwise.

1

2

Sharing the Road

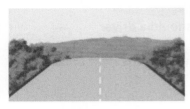

What danger should a driver allow for over the brow of this hill?
ABMW0272R

There may be a slow moving vehicle in your lane.

On the approach to the brow of a hill you should be extra careful and be prepared to react to a change in the traffic situation.

What danger should a driver allow for over the brow of this hill?
ABMW0273R

A vehicle may be broken down.

On the approach to the brow of a hill you should be extra careful and be prepared to react to a change in the traffic situation.

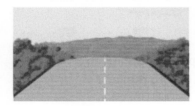

What danger should a driver allow for over the brow of this hill?
ABMW0275R

There may be oncoming pedestrians.

On the approach to the brow of a hill you should be extra careful and be prepared to react to a change in the traffic situation.

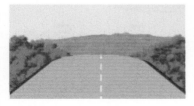

What danger should a driver allow for over the brow of this hill?
ABMW0276R

There may be livestock on the road.

On approach to the brow of a hill you should be extra careful and be prepared to react to a change in the traffic situation.

What danger should a driver allow for over the brow of this hill?
ABMW0277R

There may be hedge-cutting taking place.

On the approach to the brow of a hill you should be extra careful and be prepared to react to a change in the traffic situation.

What should a driver be aware of when following the motorcyclist, and the white car is reversing onto the road?
ABMW0282RU19

The driver following the motorcycle may need a longer braking distance than normal.

You should always keep a safe distance from the vehicle in front if it is slowing down or stopping. Always read the road and be prepared to react correctly to changes in the traffic ahead.

What should a driver do on the approach to this situation?
ABMW0283R

Reduce speed and stop if necessary.

When road priority is unclear you might have to yield to oncoming vehicles. Never drive a vehicle into an area that it might not be able to clear or where it could cause an obstruction or bottleneck.

When driving on this one-way street with vehicles parked on both sides, what should a driver be prepared for?
ABMW0288R

Pedestrians crossing between the vehicles.

When driving on a one-way street, you should be extra careful and be prepared to react to a change in the traffic situation.

What should a driver do in this situation when intending to turn left? ABMW0290RU19
Yield to pedestrians already crossing.

By law you must yield to pedestrians already crossing at a junction. Pedestrians are vulnerable road users and you should be extra careful driving at places where pedestrians are attempting to cross the road.

What should a driver do when turning right at this junction? ABMW0291R
Allow the red car to proceed.

When you are turning right from a main road into a side road, you must give way to oncoming traffic on the main road even if they are turning left into the same road.

In this situation who should wait?
The driver behind the stopped van should wait. ABMW0297R

When you are overtaking a parked vehicle or obstruction, you should yield to oncoming vehicles so that they don't have to slow down or take evasive action.

In this situation, who should wait?
The driver in the red car should wait.
ABMW0298R

A vehicle driving on the main road has priority over vehicles emerging from side roads. However, you must understand that the right of way is not an absolute right of way and you should be considerate of other road users at all times.

What should a driver who wants to turn right do in this situation? ABMW0306RU19
Proceed straight ahead or turn left.

As you approach a junction where you want to turn right, you should read the road ahead and take up the correct position for turning in good time.

Which vehicle is in the correct position to make a right turn from the major road into the minor road? MW0307R ABMW0307R
3

The correct position from which to turn right from a major road to a minor road is just left of centre. You should take up the correct position in good time and avoid cutting the corner or swan necking – that is going beyond the turning point as car 2 is in the picture.

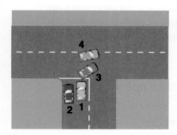

Which vehicle is in the correct position to make a right turn from a minor road onto a major road? 307R ABMW0312R
1

The correct position from which to turn right from a minor road to a major road is just left of centre of the road. You should take up the correct position in good time and complete the turn by entering the left-hand side of the major road.

What do flashing amber beacons on an oncoming vehicle alert a driver to? ABMW0323RU19
That the oncoming vehicle may be slow moving or extra wide.

Flashing amber beacons are used by recovery vehicles and vehicles carrying abnormal loads. You should be aware that these vehicles may need extra room and could conceal following traffic. When you come across such vehicles, slow down and be prepared to stop if necessary.

What should a driver do if they meet a vehicle with flashing amber beacons?

ABMW0324RU19

Slow down and prepare to stop.

Flashing amber beacons are used by recovery vehicles and vehicles carrying abnormal loads. You should be aware that these vehicles may need extra room and could conceal following traffic. When you come across such vehicles, slow down and be prepared to stop if necessary.

What should a driver do on a narrow road when another vehicle is coming in the opposite direction?

ABMW0330RU19

Reduce speed and allow reasonable clearance between their vehicle and the oncoming one before proceeding.

You should always be prepared to react to hazards ahead. When you meet a vehicle coming against you on a narrow road, you should show consideration and slow down to a appropriate speed so that the two vehicles can pass each other safely.

When a driver is driving behind another vehicle that they do not intend to overtake, what should the driver do?

ABMW0332RU19

Keep well back to allow following traffic to overtake.

You should always allow sufficient distance between your vehicle and the vehicle in front. This will enable you to stop safely (within the distance you can see clear). It will also give overtaking vehicles enough room to pull in safely to the left lane after they have passed you.

When a driver is driving in a line of traffic and does not intend to overtake, what should the driver do?

ABMW0333RU19

Stay back and leave a gap for other drivers to overtake.

You should always allow sufficient distance between your vehicle and the vehicle in front. This will enable you to stop safely (within the distance you can see clear). It will also give overtaking vehicles enough room to pull in safely to the left lane after they have passed you.

When driving into a narrow gap between oncoming vehicles and vehicles parked on the left. What should a driver do?

ABMW0342RU19

Indicate right, stopping if necessary until oncoming traffic has passed by.

When you meet approaching traffic at a narrow gap, you should show consideration and slow down to a appropriate speed so that you and the other vehicles can pass each other safely. If necessary, give way to the other vehicles.

When driving behind a heavy goods vehicle that is signalling to turn right, what should a driver do?

ABMW0350RU19

Stay behind until there is sufficient space to overtake it on the inside or until it has completed the turn.

Heavy goods vehicles need extra space on the road, and when they are turning the overhang of the vehicle may swing out into the path of overtaking or passing traffic. For that reason, it is a good idea to stay back and let the heavy goods vehicle complete its turn unless there is sufficient space to overtake safely.

When driving behind a bus that is signalling to turn left and there is oncoming traffic, what should a driver do?

ABMW0351RU19

Stay back and allow it to complete the turn.

Always allow a bus to complete a left-hand turn, because your field of view is restricted, and it could be dangerous to attempt overtaking it.

1

2

What should a driver do when driving on a wide road behind a vehicle that has signalled to turn right ahead?

ABMW0355RU19

Overtake on the left-hand side and carry on if safe to do so.

You may overtake on the left when the driver in front has moved out and signalled their intent to turn right and you intend to go straight ahead – provided there is enough room to do so safely and your path will not be obstructed by the swing of a large vehicle turning right.

When is it permissible to overtake another vehicle on the nearside (left-hand side)?

ABMW0356RU19

When the vehicle in front is signalling to turn right.

You may overtake on the left when the driver in front has moved out and signalled their intent to turn right and you intend to go straight ahead – provided there is enough room to do so safely and your path will not be obstructed by the swing of a large vehicle turning right.

What should a driver do if they are not travelling as fast as the vehicle in front?
ABMW0362RU19

The driver should keep to the left and allow vehicles to overtake if they wish.

Always read the road ahead and be prepared to react to any traffic situation. You should not drive so slowly that your vehicle unnecessarily blocks other road users. Keep as near to the left as is safe to allow other vehicles to pass safely if they wish.

What should a driver do if they wish to drive across a busy road and the traffic lights which normally control the junction are temporarily out of action?
ABMW0365RU19

Take good observation, wait for a clear break in the traffic and proceed to cross the road safely.

Always read the road ahead and be prepared to react to any traffic situation. In this case, do not proceed until it is clear and safe to do so. Do not assume that you have the right of way.

What should a driver do if they see a school bus stopped on the nearside (left side) of the road ahead?
ABMW0366RU19

Reduce speed and overtake with caution.

Always read the road and be prepared to react to any traffic situation – in this case, be aware of vulnerable road users such as school children boarding or alighting from school buses.

What should the driver do when driving behind a vehicle that is going from side to side on the road in an unsafe manner?
ABMW0367RU19

The driver should stay well back in a safe position.

You should always be prepared to react to hazards ahead. If the vehicle in front is moving from side to side, it may indicate that the driver is not paying full attention or that their driving is impaired by drink, drugs or tiredness. If you think the vehicle is a risk to the public safety, the matter should be reported to the Gardaí or to traffic watch (lo-call 1890 205 805), but not while driving.

What should a driver do if a heavy goods vehicle in front has moved out to make a left turn ahead?
ABMW0368RU19

Stay behind it and allow it to complete the turn.

Always read the road ahead and be prepared to react to any traffic situation. In this case, you should be aware that the heavy goods vehicle will need extra space to complete the left-hand turn and you should remain behind the vehicle until it has completed its turn.

What should a driver do if a bus in front has moved out to make a left-hand turn and there is oncoming traffic?
ABMW0369RU19

Stay back and allow the bus to complete the turn.

Always read the road ahead and be prepared to react to any traffic situation. In this case, you should be aware that the bus will need extra space to make the turn. So you should not overtake it if by doing so you would cause oncoming traffic to alter speed or course. Remember, you should never overtake when approaching a junction.

What should a driver do if they see a truck reversing into a side entrance on the left-hand side of the road ahead?
ABMW0370RU19

Stop back safely and wait until the way is clear.

Always read the road ahead and be prepared to react to any traffic situation. You should be aware of the difficulties that drivers of large vehicles can have reversing into a side entrance. In this case, a large vehicle reversing could obstruct your view of the road ahead as you approach, and you should afford the truck driver adequate space to manoeuvre

---

What should a driver do if they are first in line to turn right at traffic lights while the green light is showing and there is oncoming traffic approaching?
ABMW0371RU19

Go forward towards the centre of the junction and turn safely when a suitable gap appears.

If you wish to turn right at a set of traffic lights, drive into the junction when you see a green light, taking care not to block any oncoming traffic. Then complete the turn when it is safe to do so.

1
2

When is it permitted to force oncoming traffic onto the hard shoulder on the opposite side of the road while overtaking? ABMW0372R

It is not permitted to force oncoming traffic onto the hard shoulder while overtaking.

Overtaking in the manner described here is dangerous. You should overtake another vehicle only when it is safe to do so, both for you and for all other traffic. Before you overtake, make sure the road ahead is clear and that you have enough room to complete the overtaking manoeuvre and return to your own side of the road without forcing any other road user to alter speed or course.

When meeting oncoming traffic on a national road, is it permitted to move into the hard shoulder to allow following traffic to overtake?

Yes, temporarily when the hard shoulder is clear and it is safe to drive there. ABMW0374RU19

On national roads, the hard shoulder is normally for the use of pedestrians and cyclists only. If you want to allow a vehicle behind to overtake, you may pull into the hard shoulder briefly as long as no pedestrians or cyclists are using it and there are no junctions or entrances nearby. In the case of motorways, however, you must not drive on the hard shoulder, except in an emergency.

When driving on a national road is it permitted to drive on the hard shoulder in order to allow faster-moving traffic to overtake?

Yes, temporarily when the hard shoulder is clear and it is safe to drive there. ABMW0375RU19

On national roads, the hard shoulder is normally for the use of pedestrians and cyclists only. If you want to allow a vehicle behind to overtake, you may pull into the hard shoulder briefly as long as no pedestrians or cyclists are using it and there are no junctions or entrances nearby. In the case of motorways, however, you must not drive on the hard shoulder, except in an emergency.

What should a driver do in a queue of traffic controlled by traffic lights?

A driver should maintain their position in the queue. ABMW0376RU19

Always read the road ahead and be prepared to react to any traffic situation. From time to time you may have to queue in traffic. In this situation, you should try to remain patient and considerate of other road users. Jumping the queue is inconsiderate, it could be dangerous , and it could even provoke a road rage incident or cause a collision.

What should the driver do when driving a vehicle they are not familiar with?

ABMW0377RU19

Initially drive with extra care and at a lower speed until fully familiar with the vehicle.

You should know where to find and how to operate all the controls on your vehicle, including all of its safety features and warning lamps. When you are driving, you need to be able to concentrate on what's happening around you and operating the vehicle controls should be second nature to you. When you sit into the drivers seat of a vehicle you are not familiar with, you should do a thorough cockpit drill before you move off.

When stopped at traffic lights and the green light comes on, what should a driver do?

ABMW0381RU19

Check that other road users have cleared the junction and move off with care.

When stopped at traffic lights and the green light comes on, you should check to ensure the way is clear and proceed only if it is safe to do so.

What should a driver do when they get a puncture while driving?

Stop at a safe place and change the wheel.

ABMW0386RU19

If you get a puncture while driving, find a suitable and safe place to stop and change the wheel. If you cant find a suitable place immediately, drive slowly (with your hazard warning lights turned on) to avoid further damage to the tyre or rim until a safe place is found.

After overtaking another vehicle, what should a driver do?

ABMW0394RU19

Gradually move back into the left when the vehicle has been passed.

After overtaking, check your mirrors, signal and return to your normal lane position as soon as it is safe. Take a smooth easy line, gradually moving back in and allowing the other vehicle plenty of space and don't cut in sharply.

What would happen if a driver cuts in too soon when overtaking another vehicle?

ABMW0395AU19

It would force the other vehicle to suddenly slow or change direction causing danger.

When overtaking make sure the road ahead is clear so you have enough distance to overtake and get back to your own side of the road without forcing any other road user to adjust speed or direction. When you are well past the vehicle, check the mirrors, signal and gradually return to the original lane, making sure not to cut across the vehicle you have passed.

What clearance should drivers normally allow for when passing parked vehicles?

ABMW0398RU19

A door width.

When you are passing parked vehicles, you should leave at least a door's width of clearance in case somebody opens their car door unexpectedly, this will also increase visibility of pedestrians in the area.

In dry weather how might a driver judge what is a safe following distance to vehicle in front?

ABMW0427RU19

By using a fixed point and applying the two second rule.

A driver can judge a safe distance from the vehicle in front by using the two second rule, this is measured by picking a fixed point as the vehicle in front passes it begin saying "only a fool breaks the two second rule". If you pass the fixed point before you have finished the phrase, then your vehicle is too close, safely slow and increase your distance from the vehicle in front.

What phrase is recommended for drivers to help them determine a safe distance from the vehicle in front on a dry road?

ABMW0429RAU19

"Only a fool breaks the two second rule."

A driver can judge a safe distance from the vehicle in front by using the two second rule, this is measured by picking a fixed point as the vehicle in front passes it begin saying "only a fool breaks the two second rule". If you pass the fixed point before you have finished the phrase, then your vehicle is too close, safely slow and increase your distance from the vehicle in front.

When a driver wants to turn left into a property and there is a bus lane on the left, what should the driver do?
ABMW0472RU19

Give way to cyclists, taxis and buses which may be using the bus lane.

If a driver needs to cross a bus lane on their left in order to enter a property, they should take extra care that there are no buses, taxis or cyclists in the bus lane. They should check mirrors, signal and turn into the property when it is safe to do so.

What traffic may use a contra-flow bus lane?
ABMW0474U19

Buses on a scheduled service.

A contra-flow bus lane is one that runs in the opposite direction to traffic beside it. Only buses on a scheduled service may use a contra-flow bus lane.

What traffic may use a with-flow bus lane during the times specified on informaton signs at the start of the lane?
ABMW0475RU19

Buses, taxis and cyclists.

A bus lane is a special lane for the use of buses. A with-flow bus lane is one that runs in the same direction as the traffic beside it. Taxis and cyclists may also use with-flow bus lanes. Other traffic may use them outside the hours posted on the accompanying plate.

When driving along a dual carriageway in normal driving conditions, which lane should a driver be in?
ABMW0477RU19

In the left-hand lane unless the driver wishes to overtake or turn right.

You must normally drive in the left-hand lane of a dual carriageway, except when overtaking or turning right a short distance ahead.

What does a 2-plus-1 road have?
ABMW0480R

Two non-motorway lanes in one direction and one non-motorway lane in the opposite direction.

A 2-plus-1 road consists of two lanes in one direction of travel and one lane in the other direction. The two-lane section allows for safe overtaking and alternates with a one-lane section roughly every 2 kilometres.

What does a 2-plus-1 road have?

ABMW0482RU19

Two lanes of traffic in one direction and one in the opposite direction.

A 2–plus-1 road consists of two lanes in one direction of travel and one lane in the other direction. The two-lane section allows for safe overtaking and alternates with a one-lane section roughly every 2 kilometres.

Where may a driver overtake on a 2-plus-1 road?

ABMW0483R

In the two-lane stretch.

A 2-plus-1 road consists of two lanes in one direction of travel and one lane in the other direction. When you need to overtake, you should wait until you reach the 2-lane section which occurs approximately every 2 kilometres.

What should a driver do when travelling on a motorway or dual carriageway?

ABMW0484RU19

Be alert for other drivers who may suddenly change lanes or reduce speed.

Motorways and dual carriageways are designed to help traffic travel faster and more safely between destinations. Traffic conditions can change very quickly because of the speed and increased volumes of traffic and lanes, and you need to be particularly alert to other drivers changing lanes or reducing speed.

In normal driving conditions on a motorway, which lane should the driver occupy?

ABMW0485RU19

Drive in the nearside (left-hand) lane unless intending to overtake.

The normal keep left rules apply when you are driving on a motorway – a driver should stay in the nearside (left hand) lane unless they are overtaking.

What may the hard shoulder of a motorway be used for?

Stopping in an emergency.

ABMW0496RU19

There are extra dangers when driving on a motorway because of the increased volume of traffic and higher speed. For safety reasons a driver should not drive or stop on the hard shoulder of a motorway except in an emergency or breakdown.

After exiting the motorway and coming towards a junction at the end of the deceleration lane (slip road) what should a driver do? ABMW0497RU19

Be alert for oncoming and crossing traffic at the end of the slip road.

The driver should check for signs showing a lower speed; Use the speedometer to make sure that they are obeying the reduced speed limit ; remember that the slip roads and link roads between motorways may include sharp bends and that they may encounter junctions and other traffic. Remember that motorway rules no longer apply.

A driver wishes to go straight ahead at a cross junction of equal importance. If they encounter other traffic, what is the general rule that applies? ABMW0499RU19

Traffic approaching from the driver's right has right of way.

If a driver is at a junction where the roads are of equal importance, traffic on the driver's right has the right of way. The driver must let that traffic pass before moving on. It is important to understand that the right of way is not an absolute right. Drivers must proceed with caution whilst showing regard for other users of the road.

In general, when turning right on a two-way road, where should a driver position the vehicle? ABMW0513RU19

Just left of the middle of the road.

In general, the correct position to be in before turning right is just left of the centre of the road. Where the road is wide enough, this position allows traffic coming from behind and going straight ahead to pass safely on the left.The driver should be alert for road markings which direct them to follow a certain course.

What should a driver do before turning right from a major road into a minor road? ABMW0514RU19

Yield right of way to oncoming traffic and to pedestrians crossing at the junction.

The driver must yield to oncoming traffic and to pedestrians who are already crossing when turning right from a major road to a minor road.

What in particular should the driver of a large vehicle be aware of when passing pedestrians?
CD0097RU19

That the pedestrians can be affected by the vehicle's slipstream.

The driver of a large vehicle should always show due care and consideration for vulnerable road users such as pedestrians. This is particularly important in rural areas where there are no footpaths, and in bad weather. Spray, dust or debris thrown up from the wheels can make it difficult for the pedestrian to see, and the air turbulence created by the vehicle can blow them off course.

Why is a large vehicle likely to intimidate other road users?
CD0109R

The size and noise of the vehicle.

Other road users can be intimidated by the sheer size and noise of a large vehicle, but the driver should never deliberately frighten other road users, for example by revving the engine, by driving too close to them or by repeatedly pressing the footbrake to create loud hissing noises.

A driver is driving a long vehicle and wishes to turn left into a narrow side road. What should a driver do?
CD0115RU19

Move to the right on the approach to allow the turn be made without touching the pavement.

If you are driving a long vehicle and wish to turn left into a narrow road, take as much room as you need on the approach to the junction to allow you to complete the turn successfully. This may mean that your vehicle will be to the right of its normal position on the road, and other road users, especially cyclists, may come up on the inside of your vehicle.

When driving a large vehicle, why is it sometimes necessary to move to the right before making a left-hand turn?
CD0116RU19

To ensure the nearside (left side) rear wheels do not touch the kerb.

When you are turning left at a junction, steer a course that is wide enough to ensure that you do not touch the kerb with your nearside (left side) rear wheels.

When driving a large vehicle on a road which has overhanging trees, what should a driver do?
CD0120RU19

Drive in the normal position but move out as necessary to avoid hitting overhanging branches.

When driving a large vehicle on a road that has overhanging trees, maintain your normal position on the road as far as possible, but move out as necessary to avoid hitting the trees, and return to the normal position as soon as you can.

A driver is driving a large vehicle up a steep hill. There is a 'slow lane' on the left. What should the driver do?

CD0133RU19

Drive in the slow lane.

Slow lanes (also known as crawler or climbing lanes) have been introduced on some roads to allow large slower-moving vehicles get out of the way of faster-moving traffic. When driving a large vehicle, you should use such lanes where possible to help improve traffic flow.

The driver of a large vehicle needs to proceed straight ahead at a mini roundabout at which there is limited space to manoeuvre. What should the driver do?

CD0134RU19

Where possible, negotiate the mini roundabout in the same way as a normal roundabout.

Mini-roundabouts generally function as traffic calming measures. They do not always provide sufficient room for a large vehicle to negotiate them in the same way as a normal roundabout. The driver must evaluate the situation on approach and respond in a way that is appropriate for the size of their vehicle, while yielding as appropriate to other traffic.

1

2

When stopping for a short period of time in an urban area, for example to let off passengers, what should a driver do?

CD0145RU19

Avoid causing an obstruction to other road users by parking close to the left.

When stopping to pick up or let off passengers, you should stop in a location that does not cause obstruction to other road users and allows for stopping close to the kerb on the near side (left side).

What should a driver do when an emergency service vehicle approaches with flashing blue lights?

RSA0208

React quickly, safely and carefully to allow the emergency service vehicle to pass.

A driver needs to know what to do when they see an emergency vehicle. A driver must react quickly, safely and carefully to allow emergency service vehicles to pass. It is important to be alert and attentive at all times.

What should a driver never do when an emergency service vehicle approaches with flashing blue lights?

RSA0209

Brake suddenly or block the road.

A driver needs to know what to do when they see an emergency vehicle. A driver must react quickly, safely and carefully to allow emergency service vehicles to pass. It is important to be alert and attentive at all times.

Can a driver break a red light or break the speed limit to allow an emergency service vehicle to pass?

RSA0210

No, a driver should never break a red light or speed up to allow an emergency service vehicle to pass.

A driver needs to know what to do when they see an emergency vehicle. A driver must react quickly, safely and carefully to allow emergency service vehicles to pass. It is important to be alert and attentive at all times.

What is the likely effect of motorists 'rubbernecking' at the scence of a traffic incident?

RSA0215

It can cause additional incidents as drivers become distracted.

When approaching or being near to the scene of an incident, motorists are often seen 'rubbernecking'. This means turning your head and stretching your neck to get a better view of what's happening. It can be the cause of traffic jams as drivers slow down to 'rubberneck'. It can also cause road incidents as drivers become distracted and change their speed and/or direction while other drivers are also distracted.

How should a driver react to emergency services vehicles with flashing blue lights and/or sirens on?

RSA0216

Check their mirrors before looking for space to move aside.

If you see any emergency vehicle approaching with lights and/or sirens activated, check your rear view mirrors to gauge the speed of the emergency vehicle/s and also look out for pedestrians, cyclists, motorcyclists and other road users. Indicate your intention to pull over. Pull over only in a space that has enough space for the emergency vehicle/s to pass safely. Move off safely with appropriate observations and signals after the emergency vehicle has passed.

Taking Emergency / Corrective Action

What should a driver do if a front tyre bursts while driving?
ABMW0605RU19

Grip the steering wheel firmly.

If a front tyre bursts on a vehicle, the steering on the vehicle will become unstable. Dont panic – slow down gradually while keeping a firm hold on the steering wheel. Stop in a safe place to change the wheel, and alert other road users by switching on your hazard warning lights.

What precautions could a driver take against the risk of fire in their vehicle?
ABMW0607RU19

Carry a suitable fire extinguisher in the vehicle.

A strong smell of fuel is usually an indication that something is wrong, and you should stop and investigate as soon as possible. Leaking or spilling petrol can be dangerous because it is so combustible. It is good practice to carry a fire extinguisher in your vehicle, so that you can deal with any small fires

What should a driver do if their vehicle is broken down on a motorway and they are awaiting assistance?
ABMW0610U19

Switch on the vehicle hazard warning lights, get out of the vehicle and stand safely to the side.

If your vehicle breaks down on the road, always switch on the hazard warning lights and stand clear of the vehicle while awaiting assistance – this will warn other traffic that there is a vehicle stopped on the road.

How are emergency vehicles identified?
ABMW0738RU19

By flashing red or blue lights.

If you hear or see an emergency vehicle approaching sounding its siren or flashing lights, be extra careful and give way if it is safe to do so.

How should a driver apply the brakes in an emergency if the vehicle is fitted with anti-lock brakes (ABS)?
BW0135RU19

Press the brake pedal firmly and hold.

If your vehicle is fitted with ABS, brake firmly. ABS will not stop the vehicle more quickly, it will only prevent the wheels from locking. This helps you to maintain control of the vehicle.

1
2

What effect could a front-tyre blow-out have on a vehicle?

The steering wheel will pull to one side. BW0141RU19

If a front tyre on the vehicle you are driving blows out, you will feel the effect of it through the steering wheel. The wheel will generally pull to the side of the blown-out tyre.

What should a driver do when suddenly confronted by a hazard on the road?

BW0149RU19

Decelerate and apply the footbrake firmly.

To stop your vehicle in an emergency, apply the footbrake firmly, and maintain the pressure until the vehicle stops. Depress the clutch pedal just before stopping.

When driving along and required to stop suddenly, what should a driver do?

BW0150RU19

Apply the footbrake firmly.

To stop your vehicle in an emergency, apply the footbrake firmly, and maintain the pressure until the vehicle stops. Depress the clutch pedal just before stopping.

When required to stop in an emergency, what should a driver do?

Apply firm pressure on the footbrake. BW0151RU19

To stop your vehicle in an emergency, apply the footbrake firmly, and maintain the pressure until the vehicle stops. Depress the clutch pedal just before stopping.

When required to stop in an emergency, what should a driver do?

Apply the footbrake firmly. BW0152RU19

To stop your vehicle in an emergency, apply the footbrake firmly, and maintain the pressure until the vehicle stops. Depress the clutch pedal just before stopping.

What should the driver do if the service brake fails?

CPC1051

Use the secondary brake.

Combine the secondary brake with the foot brake or the parking brake control. This brake is only for use if the service brake fails. As the secondary brake normally operates on fewer wheels than the service brake it is not as effective.

Unaccompanied Driving

What is the penalty for a vehicle owner who allows a learner driver to drive their vehicle unaccompanied?
RSA0217

Their vehicle will be seized.

A learner driver needs to be aware that driving unaccompanied in a vehicle, even where the owner has given their consent to drive, may result in the vehicle being seized.

A learner permit driver who receives 7 penalty points in a 36 month period (three years) will be banned from driving for how many months?

6 months.
RSA0218

A learner driver needs to be aware that there is a lower penalty point threshold for learner or novice drivers.

What is the minimum penalty point offence for a learner driver not displaying 'L' Plates both on the front and rear of the vehicle?
RSA0219

1 penalty point.

A learner driver needs to be aware of the legal requirements to display 'L' plates front and rear and the implications of not doing so.

How many penalty points will an unaccompanied learner driver receive on conviction?
RSA0220

4 penalty points.

A learner driver needs to be aware that driving unaccompanied increases the penalty points to 4 on conviction.

What is the fine for a learner driver for driving a vehicle unaccompanied?

€120
RSA0221

A learner driver needs to be aware that driving unaccompanied increases the fine to €120 on conviction.

A learner driver who has been stopped by a Garda for driving unaccompanied faces a minimum fine of how much?

€80

A learner driver needs to be aware that, if they are stopped by a Garda for driving unaccompanied, it will lead to a financial penalty.

If the owner of a vehicle allows a learner driver to drive their vehicle, what is the maximum fine the owner could face?

€1000

A learner driver needs to be aware that driving unaccompanied in a vehicle which they do not own could see the owner facing a fine of up to €1,000 and having the vehicle seized.

Is a learner driver permitted to drive unaccompanied if they have the consent of the vehicle owner?

No, a learner driver is not permitted to drive unaccompanied even with the owner's consent.

A learner driver needs to be aware that, even with the consent of the owner of the vehicle, they are not permitted to drive unaccompanied.

For how long is a learner driver's accompanying driver required to have held their full licence in category B?

2 years.

A learner driver needs to be aware that not just anyone can be an accompanying driver. An accompanying driver has to have held a full licence for at least 2 years and have built up good driving experience.

What are the fixed charge amount and penalties incurred for a learner driver who drives unaccompanied?

€80 fine and 2 penalty points.

A learner driver needs to know that there are penalties for driving unaccompanied.

A learner driver detected of driving unaccompanied faces a minimum of how many penalty points? RSA0227

5 penalty points.

A learner driver needs to be aware that driving unaccompanied will result in a penalty point offence.

When a learner driver has passed their driving test, are they permitted to drive unaccompanied as the holder of a Certificate of Competency? RSA0228

No, a learner driver is not permitted to drive unaccompanied until they have been issued with a full driving licence in that category.

A learner driver who successfully passes their driving test needs to be aware that the rules that apply to learner permit holders still apply to them until they are in possession of a full driving licence in that category. A Certificate of Competency is not a full licence.

Can a learner driver drive unaccompanied if they are on their third or subsequent learner permit? RSA0229

No, they cannot drive unaccompanied on any learner permit.

A learner driver needs to be aware that they are not permitted under any circumstance to drive unaccompanied regardless of the amount of Learner Permits held.

Can a person who has passed their car driving test within the last two years act as an accompanying driver? RSA0230

No, they must hold the full driving licence for a minimum of 2 years.

To be an accompanying driver for a learner driver, you must have a full driving licence for at least 2 years.

Are there any occasions when a learner driver can drive unaccompanied? RSA0231

No, learner drivers must be accompanied at all times by a qualified driver.

Learner drivers must be aware that they must be accompanied by a qualified driver at all times.

Vulnerable Road Users

How can a pedestrian walking along a poorly lit road reduce the risk of an accident occuring?
RSA0213

Wear high visibility clothing.

Even with the best headlights, drivers can see less at night than during the day. Pedestrians and unlit bicycles are extremely difficult to see in the dark, particularly if they have to deal with the glare of oncoming lights. Pedestrians should always wear bright and hi-viz clothing during the day and reflective clothing at night when walking outside built-up areas.

What is a courtesy pedestrian crossing?
RSA0214

An uncontrolled pedestrian crossing place.

Pedestrians should only enter uncontrolled crossing places (courtesy crossing) ensuring that all traffic is aware of their presence if crossing the road. Motorists entering uncontrolled crossing places (courtesy crossing) should react by driving very slowly, and be aware of the potential dangers of pedestrians using the area.

Vulnerable Road Users » Cyclist

What should a driver be aware of in this situation?
ABMW0252RU19

The cyclist may move onto the roadway without paying attention to moving traffic.

You should show extra care when approaching cyclists who are about to exit from a cycle lane and join the roadway.

How should a driver overtake the cyclist in this situation?
ABMW0257R

By crossing the broken white line.

Where there are two lines in the centre of the road, you must obey the one closest to you. So, if the closest line is a broken white line, by law you may overtake, so long as it is safe to do so.

When stopped at traffic lights, a driver should take particular care for which road users coming up on their left?
ABMW0536RU19

Cyclists.

Before moving off at traffic lights and particularly when turning left you should be aware of cyclists and motorcyclists coming up on the left in general – in particular where there is an advanced stop line for cyclists ahead of that for other road users.

In slow-moving city traffic, a driver should occasionally check their blind spots for which road users in particular?
ABMW0539RU19

Cyclists.

Drivers should be aware of and check blind spots before moving off and changing direction where appropriate. Cyclists can easily become hidden in a blind spot, and in slow-moving traffic, they might be moving faster than you are.

When driving on a road that has a potholed surface and there is a cyclist ahead, what should a driver do?
ABMW0550RU19

Allow extra clearance in case the cyclist swerves to avoid a pothole.

You should always be aware of how vulnerable cyclists are. When you are driving on a road with potholes or bad surfaces, give plenty of clearance to the cyclists when overtaking them. Take into account that they may swerve suddenly to avoid potholes .

What should a driver be aware of when making a left turn into a side road?
ABMW0552RU19

Cyclists may come up on the left (nearside).

When turning left, drivers should be aware that cyclists and pedestrians may come up on the left (nearside) . Always check to your left (nearside) before you make a left turn.

What procedure should a driver follow when intending to overtake a cyclist travelling in the same direction up ahead?
ABMW0559RU19

Mirror check, indicate and move out if it is safe to do so.

The sequence drivers should follow the mirror - signal - manouvere routine when overtaking. Drivers should overtake only when it is safe to do so. Give extra space to cyclists when overtaking them, as they may need to move out to avoid a pothole, or they could be blown into your path on windy days.

When driving on dark winter mornings and evenings on unlit country roads what should a driver be aware of?

ABMW0562RU19

Cyclists are much more vulnerable in poor lighting conditions.

Drivers should take extra care when driving on dark winter mornings and evenings – vulnerable road users such as cyclists and pedestrians (particularly schoolchildren) might not be so easy to see in low light conditions.

When a driver intends to make a left-hand turn at a junction where there are pedestrians and cyclists present, what should a driver do?

ABMW19U19

Check your mirrors and watch for cyclists or pedestrians on the left.

The vehicle does not have a greater right-of-way than any other road user. As a driver you should pay particular attention to vulnerable road users such as pedestrians, cyclists and motorcyclists and be aware that they are entitled to use the road in safety.

What should a driver do when driving at night on an unlit road?

ABMW24U19

Watch out for unlit cyclists.

While driving at night and even with the best headlights, it can be very difficult to see all the hazards that you might come across – for example, stray animals or livestock on the road. At night you should drive at a speed that will enable you to stop safely within the distance you can see to be clear ahead.

When a driver intends to make a left-hand turn on a busy city street junction and there are pedestrians and cyclists around, what should the driver do?

AMBW0538RU19

Watch for cyclists or pedestrians who may try to cross the road in front of the vehicle.

When making a left-hand turn on a busy city street, drivers should pay particular attention to vulnerable road users such as pedestrians, cyclists and motorcyclists who may appear unexpectedly and may not be aware of the vehicle's intention.

What impact can a vehicle with a high cab have on the driver's ability to see other road users?

CD0143RU19

A high cab can make it more difficult to see pedestrians and cyclists around the cab area.

In a vehicle with a high cab it can be more difficult for the driver to see pedestrians and cyclists that are around the cab area. They may be out of sight below the windscreen line and/or side window line. Blind-spot and cyclops mirrors must be fitted and used particularly when moving off and in slow-moving traffic.

Which type of road users are particularly vulnerable at junctions? CD25U19
Cyclists.

Cyclists and motorcyclists are often difficult to see at junctions and may approach faster than you think.

If it is safe to overtake a cyclist in speed zones up to 50kmh, what is the recommended minimum passing distance? RSA0211
Allow a minimum of 1 metre.

A driver should drive their vehicle far enough to the left to allow traffic to safely pass or overtake on the right, but not so far to the left that you are driving on a cycle lane or blocking or endangering cyclists or pedestrians. Where a driver wishes to overtake a cyclist and it is safe to do so, they should, if it is possible, give the recommended clearance depending on the speed limit area they are in.

If it is safe to overtake a cyclist in speed zones over 50kmh, what is the recommended minimum passing distance? RSA0212
Allow a minimum of 1.5 metres.

A driver should drive their vehicle far enough to the left to allow traffic to safely pass or overtake on the right, but not so far to the left that you are driving on a cycle lane or blocking or endangering cyclists or pedestrians. Where a driver wishes to overtake a cyclist and it is safe to do so, they should, if it is possible, give the recommended clearance depending on the speed limit area they are in.

Vulnerable Road Users » Pedestrian

What should a driver be alert to in this area? ABMW0231R
Pedestrians may cross between parked cars.

When driving in a built-up area, you should drive with caution and be prepared to react to pedestrians crossing from between parked vehicles.

What should a driver do in this situation?
Allow the pedestrian to cross the road.

ABMW0302R

When approaching a zebra crossing, you must yield to pedestrians already on or about to cross the road.

There are pedestrians on the footpath ahead and there are pools of water on the road. What should a driver do?
ABMW0327R

Reduce speed and try to avoid the pools of water so as not to splash the pedestrians.

During wet conditions, you should be aware that surface water can affect the stability of your vehicle. This is particularly so where the water lies in pools. As you drive through surface water, you should show consideration to pedestrians and cyclists and try not to splash them as you pass.

When stopped at traffic lights and the green light comes on but pedestrians are still crossing the road, what should a driver do?
ABMW0528RU19

Wait as long as necessary to enable them to complete the crossing.

A green traffic light means you may go if the way is clear. If pedestrians are crossing, give way to them and let them safely cross before proceeding.

What should a driver do if the traffic light changes to green while pedestrians are still crossing at a pelican crossing?
ABMW0537RU19

Wait patiently until they have finished crossing.

A green traffic light means you may go if the way is clear. If pedestrians are crossing at a pelican crossing, give way to them and let them safely cross before proceeding.

What should a driver do if while driving they see children on the road ahead?
ABMW0545RU19

Reduce speed and be prepared to stop if necessary.

Children can be unpredictable. When driving at a higher speed and children are present, drivers must expect the unexpected, slow down and be prepared to stop if necessary.

What should a driver do when they see joggers ahead on the left?
Check the mirrors, indicate and overtake, allowing them sufficient clearance.

ABMW0549RU19

People on the road are more vulnerable than vehicles so you should treat them with extra care. If you see people jogging ahead, use the mirror–signal–manouevre routine and give plenty of clearance to the joggers when you are overtaking them.

When driving on a country road without footpaths, what should a driver expect coming towards them on their side of the road?
ABMW0556RU19
Pedestrians.

Where there is no foothpath, pedestrians are required to walk on the side of the on-coming traffic and drivers should be aware of this. Pedestrians are vulnerable road users so drivers should always be aware of their presence, especially on country roads.

What should a driver do when driving at night on an unlit road?
ABMW0557RU19
Watch out for pedestrians wearing dark clothing.

While driving at night and even with the best headlights, it can be very difficult to see all the hazards that you might come across – for example, pedestrians wearing dark clothing. As always drivers should drive at a speed that will enable them to stop safely within the distance they can see to be clear ahead.

What could happen if a driver parks on a footpath?
ABMW0558RU19
Pedestrians could be impeded.

You should never park on a footpath. Pedestrians (including people with young children in pushchairs, prams and also wheelchair users) might have to go onto the road to get around your car, and this could put them in danger.

What should a driver do when travelling on a country road with following traffic, and they meet pedestrians?
ABMW0561RU19
Signal their intention to overtake the pedestrians.

When you are driving on a road without footpaths, drivers should take extra care when they come upon pedestrians on the road. When they intend to move out and overtake, they should check the mirrors and signal to following traffic in good time to alert drivers behind that they are changing direction because of the hazard ahead.

1

2

When driving on dark winter mornings and evenings on unlit country roads, what should a driver be aware of?

ABMW0564RU19

That there could be vulnerable pedestrians walking on the road.

Drivers should take extra care when driving on dark winter mornings and evenings – vulnerable road users such as cyclists and pedestrians (particularly schoolchildren) might not be so easy to see in low light conditions.

When driving on dark winter mornings and evenings on unlit country roads, what should a driver be aware of?

ABMW0565RU19

Schoolchildren are more vulnerable on unlit country roads on dark winter mornings and evenings.

Drivers should take extra care when driving on dark winter mornings and evenings – vulnerable road users such as cyclists and pedestrians (particularly schoolchildren) might not be so easy to see in low light conditions.

At road junctions, what type of road users are particularly vulnerable?

Pedestrians.

ABMW16

Vehicles do not have an automatic right of way at junctions. As a driver you should pay particular attention to vulnerable road users such as pedestrians, cyclists and motorcyclists and be aware that they are entitled to use the road in safety.

Which of the following road users are most vulnerable in slow-moving city traffic?

ABMW22U19

Pedestrians.

In slow-moving city traffic, you should be aware of and check your blind spots before any manoeuvre. Pedestrians can easily become hidden in a blind spot, and in slow-moving traffic, they might be moving faster than you are.

When a driver meets a set of traffic lights showing green and elderly pedestrians are crossing at the junction, what should the driver do?

Allow the pedestrians to cross in their own time.

CD0175RU19

A green light is not a right of way, it is an indication that you may proceed with caution, but only if the way is clear. You must always yield to pedestrians already crossing at a junction.

Which type of road users are particularly vulnerable at junctions?
Pedestrians. CD0176R

When emerging from a junction, you should watch out for other road users such as pedestrians, who often cross at junctions. Cyclists and motorcyclists are often difficult to see at junctions and may approach faster than you think.

What road users should the driver of a large vehicle be particularly aware of on their nearside (left-hand side) at traffic lights? CD0177U19
Pedestrians.

When at traffic lights in a large vehicle, you should watch out for vulnerable road users, such as pedestrians, cyclists and motorcyclists, who may come up on your nearside (left). Check along the nearside (left) to make sure it is safe to proceed.

A driver meets a pelican crossing with a flashing amber light showing. There is a pedestrian still on the road. What should the driver do?
Wait and let the pedestrian cross at their own pace. CD0178RU19

You must yield to pedestrians at a pelican crossing when the amber light is flashing.

On average, how many pedestrians will be killed if hit by a car at 60 km/h? CPC1130U19
9 out of 10.

You should always be able to stop within a distance you can see to be clear. You need to be able to control the vehicle you are driving to the extent that you can stop without causing a problem for anyone else on the roadway. The rule means you must be alert and exercise due care and attention at all times.

On average, how many pedestrians would be killed if hit by a car at 50 km/h? CPC1131U19
5 out of 10.

You should always be able to stop within a distance you can see to be clear. You need to be able to control the vehicle you are driving to the extent that you can stop without causing a problem for anyone else on the roadway. The rule means you must be alert and exercise due care and attention at all times.

On average, how many pedestrians will be killed if hit by a car at 30 km/h? CPC1132U19

1 out of 10.

You should always be able to stop within a distance you can see to be clear. You need to be able to control the vehicle you are driving to the extent that you can stop without causing a problem for anyone else on the roadway. The rule means you must be alert and exercise due care and attention at all times.

Vulnerable Road Users » Learner Driver

What should a driver do when they see a slow moving vehicle up ahead being driven by a learner driver? ABMW0531RU19

Maintain a distance behind to avoid undue pressure.

Show patience and courtesy when driving behind a learner driver. Learner drivers are not as experienced as other road users and may drive erratically when put under pressure.

How is a learner driver likely to react in unusual traffic situations?

Slower than an experienced driver. ABMW0532RU19

You should be patient when driving behind a learner driver. Learners may not anticipate and react to unusual traffic situations as well as an experienced driver might.

Vulnerable Road Users » Motorcyclist

When negotiating junctions, which road users are particularly vulnerable? ABMW0535RU19

Motorcyclists.

Drivers should be aware that no vehicle has an automatic right of way at a junction. Drivers must pay particular attention to vulnerable road users such as motorcyclists whose presence on the road may be less visible than other vehicle types due to their smaller size or obstructions.

At traffic lights a driver should take particular care for which road users coming up on the left side (nearside)?

ABMW0541U19

Motorcyclists.

Before moving off at traffic lights you should be aware of motorcyclists unexpectedly coming up on the left hand side (nearside).

At traffic lights, a driver should take particular care for which road users coming up on the left?

ABMW18U19

Motorcyclists.

Before moving off at traffic lights the driver should be aware of traffic, particularly cyclists and motorcyclists, coming up on the left, especially where there is an advanced stop line for cyclists ahead of that which applies to other road users.

Which of the following road users are most vulnerable in slow-moving city traffic?

Motorcyclists.

ABMW21U19

In slow-moving city traffic, you should be aware of and check your blind spots before any manoeuvre. Motorcyclists can easily become hidden in a blind spot, and in slow-moving traffic, they might be moving faster than you are.

What road users should the driver of a large vehicle be particularly aware of on their nearside (left-hand side) at traffic lights?

CD26U19

Motorcyclists.

When at traffic lights in a large vehicle, you should watch out for vulnerable road users, such as pedestrians, cyclists and motorcyclists, who may come up on your nearside (left-hand side). Before moving off, check along the nearside (left-hand side) to make sure it is safe to proceed.

Control of Vehicle

Braking

What is a likely consequence of sudden braking?

ABMW0425RU19

The vehicle could be hit from behind.

As well as reading the road ahead, you should also be aware of traffic travelling behind you. This will help you react correctly in a situation where you need to brake suddenly.

If the brake pedal of a vehicle feels soft or spongy when applied, what does this mean?

ABMW0655RU19

A fault in the brake fluid system.

If the brake pedal feels soft or spongy when pressed, it could indicate that the brake fluid level is low and there is a fault in the system. Each time a driver sets out on a journey, they should test the brakes. If a fault is detected, have it checked by a competent person. Drivers should check brake fluid levels regularly.

Whilst driving, why might a driver suspect that the brake fluid level in their vehicle is low?

ABMW0656RU19

The brakes feel spongy and soft.

If the brake pedal feels soft or spongy when pressed, it could indicate that the brake fluid level is low and there is a fault in the system. Each time a driver sets out on a journey, they should test the brakes. If a fault is detected, have it checked by a competent person. Drivers should check brake fluid levels regularly.

If a driver applies the foot brake and hears a scraping noise, what is the most likely cause?

ABMW0658RU19

The brake linings or pads are worn.

Drivers should test their brakes regularly and particularly before setting out on a journey. However, if when driving they hear a scraping noise when they press the brake, the most likely reason is that the brake linings or pads are worn. In this case, brakes wont work as well as they should and the driver should have them replaced by a competent person immediately.

1
2

What may indicate a problem with the vehicle's braking system?

The vehicle's stopping ability is affected. ABMW0659RU19

Drivers should test their brakes before setting out on a journey. If when driving they notice that it is taking longer than usual to bring the vehicle to a stop, they should have the brakes checked immediatelyby a competent person.

How can a driver reduce speed without using the footbrake? CD0060RU19

By engaging the retarder.

Endurance braking systems (or retarders) are standard equipment on many trucks and buses. They enable the driver to reduce speed without using the wheel-mounted brake (or service brake). Retarders are particularly useful when descending hills, as they help to extend the life of the brakes and to prevent brake fade.

Given similar road conditions and vehicle speeds, what braking distances will a truck or bus/minibus need compared to a car? CD0061RU19

Longer distances.

When driving a car on a good road in good weather, the driver should leave at least a 2-second gap between them and the vehicle in front. A larger vehicle needs a bigger gap, because of its greater weight and momentum. The driver should allow at least a 4-second gap under normal conditions, and even more on wet or icy roads.

Controlling vehicle stability

To secure loose bulk loads (e.g. sand) which of the following should be used? C1323

Sheeting cover.

Loose bulk loads, such as sand, are typically not packaged and are usually carried in open-bodied vehicles. As they are susceptible to displacement and blowing away, a suitable cover, such as sheeting, should be used to cover and protect the load.

What should a driver engage to assist traction when approaching a muddy surface? C1311U19

Diff-lock.

Engaging the diff-lock ensures that power is transmitted to all driven wheels. This aids traction on surfaces such as mud or snow.

What is the purpose of a diff-lock?

CD0079RU19

It improves traction on soft ground.

A driving axle is fitted with a differential, which allows the wheels on either side to rotate at different speeds, so that the vehicle can negotiate bends and corners. The purpose of a diff-lock is to cause the wheels to rotate at the same speed, and this is used when extra traction is required, for example if the vehicle is stuck in mud or snow. The diff-lock should be used only at low speed and should be disengaged as soon as possible.

When should a driver use a diff-lock on a truck?

CD0080R

When stuck on soft ground.

A driving axle is fitted with a differential, which allows the wheels on either side to rotate at different speeds, so that the vehicle can negotiate bends and corners. The purpose of a diff-lock is to cause the wheels to rotate at the same speed, and this is used when extra traction is required, for example if the vehicle is stuck in mud or snow. The diff-lock should be used only at low speed and should be disengaged as soon as possible.

When should a driver use a diff-lock in a truck?

CD0081R

When stuck on snow or ice.

A driving axle is fitted with a differential, which allows the wheels on either side to rotate at different speeds, so that the vehicle can negotiate bends and corners. The purpose of a diff-lock is to cause the wheels to rotate at the same speed, and this is used when extra traction is required, for example if the vehicle is stuck in mud or snow. The diff-lock should be used only at low speed and should be disengaged as soon as possible.

The diff-lock has been engaged to enable a truck to move off on a slippery road surface. When should the driver disengage it?

CD0082R

As soon as the truck is underway.

A driving axle is fitted with a differential, which allows the wheels on either side to rotate at different speeds, so that the vehicle can negotiate bends and corners. The purpose of a diff-lock is to cause the wheels to rotate at the same speed, and this is used when extra traction is required, for example if the vehicle is stuck in mud or snow. The diff-lock should be used only at low speed and should be disengaged as soon as possible.

Pre-Start Routine

When adjusting the driver's seat, the driver needs to ensure which of the following? CD1343

They can reach the pedals easily.

The driver's seat should be adjusted such that the driver is comfortable, has good visibility and can reach the pedals and hand controls easily.

To ensure an ergonomically sound driving position, drivers should ensure which of the following are adjusted correctly? CD1345U19

Mirrors.

All mirrors should be adjusted so that they can be viewed correctly and without strain.

Which of the following is most likely to cause a driver to experience aching shoulders, arms and back after a long drive? CD1346U19

Poor posture.

A poor driving position and posture may cause a driver to experience aching shoulders, arms and back after a long drive.

Which of the following must a driver do when carrying out a cockpit drill? RSA01032U19

Check that all mirrors are correctly aligned.

As part of the drivers cockpit drill they must check that the mirrors are properly aligned on a bus before starting a journey.

Which of the following are essential internal PSV checks required prior to driving a bus? RSA01035U19

That Fire extinguisher, first aid kit, emergency hammer are in place and serviceable.

Under Health and safety these items are required in case of an emergency.

1

2

Which of the following is an essential PSV check required prior to driving a bus?
RSA01036U19

Check that the emergency exit door operates freely and that the buzzer sounds.

Under Health and safety the emergency door must be clearly marked and accessible at all time. It must never have locks on it or be locked/restricted at any time as it is required in case of an emergency.

Which of the following is an essential interior PSV walk around check required on a bus?
RSA01037U19

Passenger safety belts, seats, handrails, walkways, lighting and luggage racks are in good condition.

Essential interior PSV walkaround checks include that passenger safety belts are operating, have no cuts or fraying. Seats should be fixed in place, not broken in anyway. Handrails should have no sharp edges and should be fixed in place. Walkways should be clear and carpets fixed in place. There should be no uneven surfaces liable to cause tripping. Lighting must be working to give clear walkways. Luggage racks must be fixed in place with secure restraints.

1
2

When must a bus driver ensure when carrying out a cockpit drill?

That there is good visibility for the driver through the bus windows and from the mirrors.
RSA01038U19

When carrying out a cockpit drill bus drivers must check that they have good all round visibility through the windows and from the mirrors. The bus driver should not move the vehicle until the checks have been carried out. The bus driver must have all round visibility.

Which of the following is included in the drivers cockpit drill?
RSA01042U19

Proper adjustment of the driving controls, seat and driver safety belt.

All controls must be working correctly to drive the bus safely and the driver must be secure in his seat and be able to control the bus safely from his seat.

Which of the following must a driver check when carrying out a bus cockpit drill?
RSA01043U19

That the windscreen washer, wipers, demister and horn are operating correctly.

When carrying out a cockpit drill bus drivers must check that That the windscreen washer, wipers, demister and horn are operating correctly. The bus driver should not move the vehicle until all the checks have been carried out.

Primary Controls

What can cause a vehicle to skid?

ABMW31U19

Excessive heavy braking.

Heavy braking can cause a vehicle to skid, particularly if the road surface is wet or uneven, or if the tyres are worn or incorrectly inflated. Read the road well ahead and try to avoid heavy braking, particularly in wet or slippery conditions.

The parking brake (hand brake) generally works on which wheels?

The rear wheels.

BW0079RU19

In most vehicles, the parking brake operates on the rear wheels only. The function of the parking brake (handbrake) is to stop the vehicle from moving when it is parked or when it is stopped on a hill. Drivers normally use the parking brake when the vehicle is already stationary and should generally not use it to stop the vehicle. It is even more important to use the parking brake when parked on a hill or when stationary in a vehicle with automatic transmission to prevent creep.

What is the purpose of a 'range-change' gearbox?

C0032R

It offers the driver a selection of high and low gears to suit the load being carried or the terrain.

A 'range-change' gearbox offers a wider range of gears than a standard gearbox. By offering the choice of high or low ratios, it effectively doubles the number of gears available, so that the driver can choose the most appropriate gear for the road and the load being carried.

What is the effect of a two-speed axle?

C1310U19

It doubles the number of ratios available to the driver.

A two-speed axle is a system whereby an electrical switch activates a mechanism in the rear axle that doubles the number of ratios available to the driver.

When driving an unfamiliar vehicle, what should a driver pay particular attention to?

CD0112RU19

That the height, weight, length and width and the controls may differ from the vehicle usually driven by the driver.

If you are required to drive a vehicle with which you are unfamiliar, you should take time to familiarise yourself with the controls and operating systems. You should also learn the height, length, width and weight of the vehicle, so that you can comply with any restrictions you meet on the road.

Technical
Matters

Braking Systems

What does Anti-lock braking system (ABS) do? ABMW0654U19

ABS prevents the wheels from locking under harsh braking conditions.

Anti-lock braking system (ABS) is a type of braking system found in most modern cars. It comes into play automatically when the driver brakes harshly. In the wet it can help prevent the wheels from skidding so that, if necessary, the driver can continue to steer while braking. Be aware that ABS does not reduce the braking distance.

What can be affected by driving on under-inflated tyres? ABMW27U19

Braking ability.

Under-inflated tyres may adversely affect many of the vehicles systems, including its braking ability, suspension, steering and fuel consumption. In particular, under-inflated tyres can affect the vehicles braking ability and can result in premature tyre wear. Tyres should always be inflated according to the vehicle manufacturers guidelines, information on which can be found in the vehicle handbook.

In general, above what gross vehicle weight must a trailer have brakes fitted? BW0080RU19

750 kg

Brakes must be fitted to a trailer if its gross vehicle weight exceeds either 750kg or half the weight of the towing vehicle.

What does a warning buzzer in the cab usually indicate? C0028RU19

Drop in brake air pressure in the braking system.

Vehicles fitted with air brakes are equipped with a buzzer to alert the driver to a loss of air pressure. You should not attempt to drive while this buzzer is sounding. If the buzzer comes on when you are driving, pull over in a safe place as soon as possible. If your vehicle loses all air pressure, the brakes may lock on, which may cause an obstruction or hazard to other traffic.

What does an unloader valve do? C0034R

It releases excess air pressure in the braking system.

An unloader valve prevents the build-up of excess pressure in the air tanks of a vehicle fitted with air brakes. The valve is fitted between the compressor and the air tanks. It opens and closes at pre-set pressures, and you will hear a change in the sound of the compressor as it operates.

What is an unloader device valve fitted to?

C1308U19

Air brake system.

An unloader valve is a device fitted to air brake systems, pre-set to operate as sufficient pressure is achieved and allowing the excess to be released.

On a vehicle equipped with an air-brake system, what is an indication of low air-pressure?

CD0062RU19

A warning light comes on and/or a buzzer sounds in the cab.

Most modern HGVs and buses are fitted with air brakes. If air pressure drops in the braking system, a warning light and/or buzzer alerts the driver. The driver should pull in and stop safely before total loss of air pressure. Other examples could be that the air pressure gauge shows insufficient pressure and there could be a sound of an air leak.

What does a load-sensing valve do?

CD0071

Adjusts the brake pressure which is applied at the wheels.

A load-sensing valve regulates the pressure passing to the brakes, so that maximum pressure is available only when the vehicle is fully laden. As the load on the vehicle reduces, the valve automatically lowers the braking pressure.

Where is the air that is used in the air brake systems stored?

CPC1028U19

Reservoir tanks.

The air reservoir holds the compressed or pressurised air.

How do endurance braking systems control vehicle speed?

CPC1029U19

Without the need for using wheel-mounted brakes.

Endurance braking systems help to control vehicle speed without using wheel-mounted brakes which operate on the principle of friction. This will apply resistance via the transmission to the rotation of the vehicles driven wheels.

How does the driver know that a vehicle's anti-lock braking system (ABS) is faulty?
CPC1032U19

A warning light will come on.

ABS activates automatically. It prevents the wheels from locking so that the driver can continue to steer the vehicle while braking. ABS is only a driver aid. It does not help the vehicle to stop more quickly. A constantly lit ABS light may indicate a fault with the braking system.

What system helps to reduce brake fade due to high brake component temperatures?
CPC1036U19

Endurance braking system.

Endurance braking systems help to control vehicle speed without using wheel-mounted brakes which operate on the principle of friction. This will apply resistance via the transmission to the rotation of the vehicles driven wheels.

Which system uses exhaust braking to slow a vehicle?
CPC1037U19

Retarders.

Retarders can be mechanical, electrical or hydraulic. Mechanical retarders can alter the engine exhaust flow to slow the vehicle without using wheel-mounted brakes. This is called exhaust braking.

In what situation are endurance braking systems especially useful?
CPC1046U19

Going down long hills.

Endurance brakes/retarders can be particularly useful on the descent of long hills, when the vehicle speed can be controlled without using the service brakes.

When travelling down a hill, how should a driver regulate their speed?
CPC1048U19

By first using the service brake to slow the vehicle.

In order to maintain control of the vehicle, all actions must be considered carefully, and the driver must ensure that all braking is done in good time and in a controlled manner.

Which of the following can occur if the driver constantly applies the brakes on a long downhill stretch?
CPC1049AU19

Brake fade

Continuous use of brakes results in them becoming overheated and losing their effectiveness. Avoiding prolonged harsh braking reducing the effects of brake fade.

What can cause ice to form in the valves and pipes of air brake systems?

Moisture in the air system coupled with freezing temperatures.
CPC1053U19

In cold weather, moisture which condenses in the air reservoirs can lead to ice forming in valves and pipes and may result in air pressure loss and/or system failure.

What happens when air pressure drops below normal in one of the brake reservoirs?
CPC1054U19

A warning light comes on.

Air warning lights or buzzer will activate when there is a drop in brake air pressure.

1

2

Vehicle Mechanics

When a driver operates the indicator switch and hears a more rapid clicking noise than normal, what could this mean?
ABMW0653RU19

An indicator bulb may have blown.

A rapid clicking noise when you turn on an indicator is usually a sign that one of the indicator bulbs has failed. Drivers are responsible for making sure that their vehicle is roadworthy. This should include a regular check that all lights, reflectors and indicators, are working properly.

If the oil pressure gauge shows little or no pressure, or the warning light comes on, what could the problem be?
ABMW0665RU19

The oil level is too low.

Drivers should check the oil level in their vehicle regularly, and if it is low, top it up. If it needs to be topped up very often, have the vehicle checked by a competent person to see if there is a problem.

What may happen if the vehicle's engine oil is not changed as required?

Parts of the engine may suffer increased wear.
ABMW0666RU19

Engine oil becomes inefficient over time losing its viscosity and lubricating qualities and therefore must be changed as required in accordance with the manufacturer's recommendations. Failure to do so may result in costly and extensive engine damage. The oil change is usually done when the vehicle is being serviced.

If a vehicle is driven with low oil pressure, what effect does this have on its engine?
ABMW0667RU19

It increases wear and tear on the engine.

Low oil pressure is usually related to low oil level or to a faulty oil pump. Low engine oil level should be topped up in accordance with the manufacturer's recommendations. Failure to do so may result in costly and extensive engine damage.

If the vehicle's oil-pressure gauge is reading low or the red oil-pressure warning light comes on, what should a driver do?

ABMW0668RU19

Drive to a safe place, stop the vehicle and check the oil level.

Oil circulation is essential for the safe running of the vehicles engine. If the warning lights or gauges indicate that the oil or the oil-pressure is low, the driver should stop as soon as they can in safe place, check the oil level, and top up if necessary. Continuing to drive may damage the engine. If the problem is not just related to the oil level, have the vehicle checked by a competent person.

What should a driver do before checking the engine oil level on a vehicle?

ABMW0669RU19

Make sure that the engine is switched off and cold.

Drivers need a basic knowledge of the regular checks that should be carried out on their vehicle. Checking the engine oil level is important – do this with the vehicle parked on level ground with the engine switched off and cold for a more accurate reading. Refer to the vehicle handbook for further information and guidance.

What is the purpose of engine oil?

ABMW0670RU19

It lubricates the engine.

The purpose of engine oil is to lubricate and cool the moving parts of the engine. Refer to the vehicle handbook for further information and guidance.

When is it recommended to use coolant?

ABMW0673RU19

All year round.

The purpose of coolant is to keep the engine cool during operation. Coolant is usually a mixture of water and anti-freeze – this ensures that the engine is kept cool and that the coolant does not freeze in very cold weather.

What happens if the vehicle has a flat battery?
ABMW0675RU19

The engine will not start.

All motor vehicles have a battery to supply power, primarily to start the engine. If the battery is flat, the driver will not be able to start the engine in the normal way. When the engine is running, it produces its own electricity to recharge the battery and run the various electrical components, including lights, heating, the radio and so on. If the battery is completely dead it will have to be replaced.

What is the primary purpose of the battery fitted to a petrol - or diesel - powered motor vehicle?
ABMW0676RU19

To start the engine.

The primary purpose of the battery is to start the engine. When the engine is running, it produces its own electricity to charge the battery and run the various electrical components, including lights, heating, radio and so on.

What effect would a weak battery have on a vehicle's driving performance?
ABMW0681RU19

It would have no effect.

It might be difficult to start a car with a weak battery, but once the engine is running, it makes no difference. If the battery fails to charge or maintain its full charge seek advice from a competent person.

What effect can a worn shock absorber have on a vehicle?
ABMW0682RU19

It can cause the vehicle to 'bounce' in an unstable manner.

A worn shock absorber can seriously affect the control of the vehicle especially on uneven surfaces or when cornering and can cause unnecessary wear and tear on tyres. It may increase stopping distance by not keeping the tyres in proper contact with the road under harsh braking.

Why should the valve be replaced when having a tubeless tyre fitted?
ABMW0693RU19

To ensure the tyre will remain inflated.

When fitting a new tubeless tyre to a vehicle it is recommended to change the valve. This is because the old valve has been on the wheel since the old tyre was fitted. The old valve may break down, leak or cause air to escape.

What effect does low tyre-pressure have on a vehicle?
Braking and cornering are impaired.   ABMW0701RU19

Incorrect tyre pressure adversely affects many of a vehicles systems, including suspension, steering and fuel consumption. In particular, under-inflated tyres can affect the vehicles braking ability and its effectiveness when cornering. Tyres should always be inflated according to the vehicle manufacturers guidelines, information on which can be found in the vehicle handbook.

What is an effect of under-inflated tyres on a vehicle?   ABMW0708RU19
Impaired braking and steering.

Drivers should check their vehicles tyre pressures (including the spare) regularly at least once a week. Under-inflated tyres adversely affect many of a vehicles systems, including braking ability, suspension, steering, fuel consumption and premature tyre wear. Tyres should always be inflated according to the vehicle manufacturers guidelines, information on which can be found in the vehicle handbook.

While driving at higher speeds, what does a continuous vibration in the steering indicate?
The wheel balance is uneven.   ABMW0713RU19

If a driver feels a continuous vibration in the steering, particularly at higher speeds, this could typically indicate that the balance of the vehicle wheels is uneven. This can lead to instability in the handling of the vehicle. If this is the case, have it investigated by a competent person.

After changing a wheel on a vehicle, which of the following should be checked after a short distance?
The wheel nut tightness.   ABMW26U19

After changing a wheel on a vehicle, check the tightness of the wheel nuts or studs on the replacement wheel after driving a short distance to ensure they are securely fitted. If in doubt seek assistance from a competent person.

What is the advantage of a two-speed axle?
C0033R

It doubles the number of gear ratios available to a driver.

A two-speed axle doubles the number of gear ratios available to the driver by offering a choice of two final drive ratios in the rear axle. The selection is made by operating an electrical switch.

What does 'road-friendly' suspension do?
CD0072R

Reduces the impact of a vehicle's weight on the road.

Road-friendly suspension, also known as air suspension, protects the load in a vehicle by reducing vibration. It can also reduce the damage to road surfaces and bridges caused by heavy loads.

What would be the likely effect of a defect in the power steering system?

It could make the steering seem heavy and stiff to turn.
CD0073U19

When the power assistance is in correct operation, the steering does not have too much play and operates freely.

What would indicate to the driver that there was a problem with the power steering?
CD0075U19

An inability to easily turn the steering wheel.

Power steering is a system that reduces the effort that a driver needs to turn the front wheels. It generally consists of a fluid reservoir and a hydraulic pump powered by the engine. If the pump malfunctions or the fluid level drops, steering the vehicle may become very difficult.

What is the function of the transmission system in a truck or bus? CD0088RU19

To transmit power from the engine to the wheels.

The transmission system of the vehicle is made up of the clutch, gearbox and driveshafts. Torque power is transmitted from the engine to the road wheels via the clutch, gearbox and driveshafts to make the vehicle move.

How is power transmitted from the engine and eventually to the road wheels?
CPC1007U19

By the gearbox and drive shaft.

Power and torque is the method of transmitting the power from the engine to the road wheels.

What is the primary function of the instrument in the picture above?
CPC1010U19

To help the driver to select the most appropriate throttle and gear setting.

This is a rev which indicates engine revolutions.

Look at the picture below. When the needle moves from 10 to 20, what does this indicate an increase in?

Engine revolutions.
CPC1012U19

The rev counter demonstrates the rotation of the crank shaft through 360 degree rotation, better know as revolution counter.

Why is AdBlue or Diesel Exhaust Fluid added to the fuel system?
It reduces the oxides of ammonia in diesel fuel emissions.
RSA01033U19

Diesel engines are now required to meet strict Nitrogen Oxide (Nox) emissions standards to help control air pollution. Adblue assists in lowering the release of harmful emissions into the environment.

Why should you monitor the levels of AdBlue or Diesel Exhaust Fluid?
It reduces the oxides of ammonia in diesel fuel emissions.
RSA01034U19

Diesel engines are now required to meet strict Nitrogen Oxide (Nox) emissions standards to help control air pollution. Adblue assists in lowering the release of harmful emissions into the environment.

Vehicle Specifications

What is the Maximum Authorised Mass (M.A.M) in tonnes of a 4-axle rigid truck with conventional (non air) suspension?
C0018AA

30 Tonnes.

The maximum permitted laden weight of a 4-axle rigid truck with conventional suspension is 30 tonnes. Overloading any truck is illegal and can have serious consequences.

What is the Maximum Authorised Mass (M.A.M) in tonnes of a 4-axle rigid truck with road friendly (air) suspension?
C0019A

32 Tonnes.

The maximum permitted laden weight of a 4-axle rigid truck with road-friendly suspension is 32 tonnes. Overloading any truck is illegal and can have serious consequences.

What is the Maximum Authorised Mass (M.A.M) in tonnes of a 3-axle rigid truck with conventional (non air) suspension?
C0020A

25 Tonnes.

The maximum permitted laden weight of a 3-axle rigid truck with conventional suspension is 25 tonnes. Overloading any truck is illegal and can have serious consequences.

What is the Maximum Authorised Mass (M.A.M) in tonnes of a 2-axle rigid truck with conventional suspension?
C0021AA

18 Tonnes.

The maximum permitted laden weight of a 2-axle rigid truck with conventional suspension is 18 tonnes. Overloading any truck is illegal and can have serious consequences.

When can a vehicles maximum axle weight be exceeded?
C0050RU19

It can never be exceeded.

The maximum design weight of the axle must never be exceeded. To do so is illegal, would negatively affect the stability and braking distance and may cause damage to the vehicle and road surface.

Why is it important to distribute the weight evenly between the axles when loading a heavy goods vehicle?

C0059RU19

To ensure maximum stability.

A driver should ensure that the load is evenly distributed to ensure the stability of the vehicle. In addition, the load should be secured against the headboard to prevent it from moving forward under braking, and heavy items should be placed at the bottom to prevent the vehicle from becoming top-heavy.

How should the load on a vehicle be arranged to maintain a safe centre of gravity?

C1321U19

As low as possible.

Ensuring that the load centre of gravity is as low as possible helps ensure the vehicles stability. A load with a high centre of gravity is less secure and can cause the vehicle to topple.

What is the maximum permitted rear load overhang that does not require a red flag or marker?

CD0042A

1 metre.

In order to warn other road users, loads extending from the rear of a vehicle by more than 1 metre must be clearly marked with a red flag or marker by day and by a lamp by night. The overhang must not exceed 3 metres.

What is the maximum permitted rear load overhang with a red flag?

3 metres.

CD0043

In order to warn other road users, loads extending from the rear of a vehicle by more than 1 metre must be clearly marked with a red flag or marker by day and by a lamp by night. The overhang must not exceed 3 metres.

What is the maximum permitted rear load overhang that does not require a red flag or marker?

CD0044R

1 metre.

In order to warn other road users, loads extending from the rear of a vehicle by more than 1 metre must be clearly marked with a red flag or marker by day and by a lamp by night. The overhang must not exceed 3 metres.

When is a red flag a sufficient marker for a rear-load overhang that exceeds one metre?

CD0045U19

Only during the day.

In order to warn other road users, loads extending from the rear of a vehicle by more than 1 metre must be clearly marked with a red flag or marker by day and by a lamp by night. The overhang must not exceed 3 metres.

What is the maximum permitted side-load overhang in millimetres?

305mm.

CD0046R

The maximum side-load overhang normally permitted is 305 millimetres (1 foot). To carry a load with a greater overhang, you need an abnormal load permit, which can be obtained from An Garda Síochána.

What is the maximum permitted length of an articulated vehicle?

16.5 metres.

CD0047R

The maximum permitted length of an articulated vehicle is 16.5 metres. To drive a longer vehicle or load, you must apply for permits from the Local Authorities of the areas through which you will be driving and/or An Garda Síochána.

What is the maximum width of a bus?

D0017RU19

2.55 metres.

Knowing the width of your bus will help when it comes to manoeuvring in tight spaces - for example, when you are parking, emerging from an exit or reversing into a garage or bus station bay.

What is the maximum height of a double-decker bus?

D0018R

4.57 metres.

You should always know the height of your vehicle, and bear it in mind when driving in areas with restricted heights, such as low and arch bridges, and bus garage doors. A collision could result in serious or fatal injury to passengers. The maximum permitted height is 4.57 metres.

What is the maximum permitted length of a two-axle bus?

D1300U19

13.5 metres.

Drivers should always know the number of axles and the length of their vehicle to ensure proper weight distribution. They need to bear it in mind when required to judge safe distances, for example for overtaking. The maximum permitted length of a bus which has two axles is 13.5 metres.

What is the maximum permitted length of a bus having more than two axles?

D1301U19

15 metres.

Drivers should always know the number of axles and the length of their vehicle to ensure proper weight distribution. They need to bear it in mind when required to judge safe distances, for example for overtaking. The maximum permitted length of a bus which has more than two axles is 15 metres.

What is the maximum permitted length of an articulated bus?

D1302U19

18.75 metres.

Drivers should always know the length of their vehicle. They need to bear it in mind when negotiating tighter areas and spaces. They are also required to judge safe distances, for example for overtaking. The maximum permitted length of an articulated bus is 18.75 metres.

In calculating the laden weight of a large public service vehicle, the vehicle is deemed to be carrying its full complement of standing and sitting passengers when a weight of how many kilos is placed in the correct relative positions?

D1305U19

65 kg.

A driver should be aware of the weight of their vehicle and any load carried. Overloading any vehicle is illegal and can have serious consequences.

Case Studies
Trucks

1
2

Case Study No.1

Gavin drove a refrigerated truck for Pugh's Produce. He was responsible for delivering fresh produce to supermarkets around Ireland. This morning, Gavin's job was to drive from Dublin to Cork with a large truck full of crates of lettuce. He had a scheduled "delivery window" of noon to 1:00 pm. After loading the crates into the truck and stacking them evenly and at a low level, Gavin calculated the weight of the truck with the crates. He was satisfied that the weight was under the maximum permitted axle weight and gross vehicle weight (GVW).

Gavin performed the daily walk-around and cockpit checks of his vehicle. He checked the following:

Gavin found everything to be in order after he completed his checks. As he inserted his tachograph chart, he remembered that he needed to get another tachograph calibration certificate as his was issued seven years ago. He was not going to do that today. He hoped that he would not have to provide his certificate for inspection on this delivery.

Gavin's Walk-Around Check
Brakes
Lights & Indicators
Tyres & Wheel Securing
  Nuts and Markers
Mirrors/Glass
Speedometer
Tachograph
Number Plates
Reflectors
Exhaust System
Correct plating
Current Test Certificate
Insurance
Seat Belts
Load Being Carried

Gavin's Cockpit Drill
Doors
Seat
Handbrake
Mirrors
Fuel

Gavin began his journey mid-morning feeling relaxed, refreshed, and fully alert. From his years as a professional truck driver, he had learned to get adequate rest before a long drive. His delivery destination in Cork was about 250 kilometres away. Gavin knew that his progress would be delayed because the number of trucks on the roads had increased in recent years. Taking into account unloading time, he hoped to reach home by mid-afternoon.

On this trip Gavin would have to travel on his least favourite route, which was a long stretch of a single lane road. While on the road, he came upon a car going significantly under the speed limit. Since the car was travelling slowly and the oncoming lane was clear, Gavin decided to pass the vehicle. He signalled, overtook the car, quickly switched back into the correct lane, and checked his mirrors. However, he did not immediately see the car in his mirrors when he switched back into the correct lane.

At one point during the trip, Gavin was not paying close attention to the road and suddenly realised that he had to make a quick left turn to keep on his route. He hit the brakes but still took the corner very fast. The pressure of the turn caused the trailer door to open. Some of the heads of lettuce rolled out onto the road, indicating that one of the crates had opened and spilled due to an obviously unsecured door. Gavin knew he had to pull over and assess the situation. Not seeing any "No Parking" signs, he parked on the left side of the road, parallel with the kerb. Since the ground was level, he put the transmission into neutral, got out of the cab, and headed to the back of the truck to assess the situation. As he secured the cargo and door, he remembered that he had not checked the rear doors before starting his journey.

Fortunately, there were no other vehicles following him when he had turned left. Gavin was able to collect the lettuce that had spilled onto the road. He decided he would dispose of it at his next stop. He was grateful that he was not responsible for the lettuce that had been damaged.

As Gavin drove into Cork, the traffic was heavy and it was raining hard. He kept the same separation distance from the car ahead of him as he had before it began raining. He was thankful that he had made good time before the rain started. He knew he was well within the scheduled delivery window. It looked like he would get home in the afternoon as he had planned. Gavin arrived at the supermarket at 12:30 pm.

Case Study No.2

Jim drove heavy vehicles and tankers for the past 10 years and was qualified for International Carriage of Dangerous Goods by Road (ADR) Class 3 goods for the past seven years. This morning, Jim's job was to take an empty tanker to a fuel distribution depot. He collected his documentation from the traffic clerk and made sure he was carrying his ADR authorisation and driver's digital tachograph card. He downloaded the card only five days ago (his truck was fitted with a digital tachograph). Jim needed both documents today because of the type of work he was doing.

After completing his vehicle checks and "nil defect" report form, Jim checked all the safety equipment to make sure it complied with his ADR authorisation. He drove to the fuel depot with the empty tanker. The tanker was a rigid four-axle, fitted with single wheels providing extended tracking width. It had road-friendly suspension, a design gross vehicle weight (DGVW) of 32,000 kilograms, was 3.7 metres high, and had the most up-to-date tanker specifications and fuel compartments.

Jim arrived at the fuel distribution depot and complied with all the site and safety regulations pointed out by the depot supervisor. He noticed the familiar difference in how the truck handled with the full load of liquid, especially if he relaxed the footbrake when stopping. Today, Jim was to deliver a load of diesel to a large haulage yard. He had delivered to this yard before so he was able to carefully plan his route. The direct route to the haulage yard had a bridge with a weight restriction of 20,000 kilograms. There was also a low bridge just before the haulage yard.

On his way, Jim came across a road block with a detour sign that directed him onto an unfamiliar road. He knew the detour would add time to his route so he picked up speed. While driving around a sharp right-hand bend in the road he hit the brakes lightly. When he felt the wheels begin to lift slightly, he took his foot off the accelerator and drove to the outside of the bend. He then felt the wheels firmly on the road again. However, his relief was short-lived.

Continuing on, Jim arrived at the foot of a long, steep incline. Halfway up the hill he noticed a sign at a junction which indicated that no large goods vehicles (LGVs) with three or more axles were allowed. He knew that the detour route would be the shortest way back to his planned route so he decided to ignore the sign. Soon enough, he joined up with his planned route.

When Jim arrived at the haulage operator's yard he braked to a stop. Just before he came to a final halt, he relaxed the brakes and felt a sudden force acting on his truck.

The operator asked him to dispense half the load at the site and deliver the other half to a different site. Jim agreed and carefully dispensed the fuel evenly from the correct compartments. However, he failed to notice an initial spillage. He then drove to his final drop-off point and unloaded the remaining fuel.

1
2

Case Study No.3

Graham was an owner-operator who lived in Dublin and typically hauled a variety of goods. On this trip, he planned to deliver pallets of various products. The estimated road time for the journey would be three days. Graham had just taken his weekly rest of 45 hours and planned to head out early Monday morning. He wanted to make good time so that he could eat dinner at a reasonable hour, enjoy a restful night's sleep, and get another early start on Tuesday.

Graham was driving a three-axle truck with road-friendly suspension and a design gross vehicle weight (DGVW) of 24 tonnes. He checked the plate and calculated the weight to make sure his vehicle was not overloaded. This was a real concern to Graham as he had broken this rule on his last trip. To make matters worse, he was also involved in a minor accident on that trip. Even though Graham did not damage the front of his cab or the back of the truck that he hit, he reported the accident to his insurance company, just to be on the safe side. Graham and his insurance agent then realised that, during that trip, his load had exceeded the legal weight. He remembered the stress the situation had caused him. He did not want to go through that worry again.

Since Graham would be hauling to Spain and his combined weight with the load would be about 24 tonnes, he checked all of his paperwork. He made sure that he had the proper licence, consignment note, and other required documentation with him in his truck. He also remembered to double-check the issue date of his National Road Haulage Operator's Licence as he knew it would be expiring the following month. Graham confirmed that all his papers were in order. He then went through each item on his systems checklist and verified that everything on the list was in working order.

Graham loaded the 22 Euro pallet for delivery and double-checked that the pallets had not shifted. He also checked that the lashings were in good condition and attached at the proper anchorage points even though he knew he would be checking them again after a few kilometres. One of the pallet lashings had been shortened due to previous damage so Graham attached it to a strap holding the cargo to a pallet. Finally, he covered the cargo with load sheets, attached the webbing straps, and did a check of the sheeting and roping before tucking a loose rope end next to a rear light under the sheet.

Graham was on the road at 7:00 am on Monday morning. By noon, he was hungry and stopped to eat a quick lunch. After finishing and paying for his meal, he

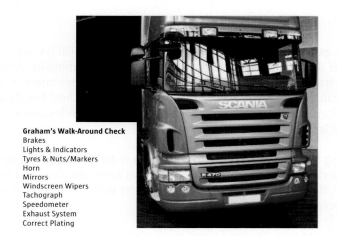

Graham's Walk-Around Check
Brakes
Lights & Indicators
Tyres & Nuts/Markers
Horn
Mirrors
Windscreen Wipers
Tachograph
Speedometer
Exhaust System
Correct Plating

climbed into the truck cab for the last leg of that day's trip. He checked his watch and noticed it was 1:00 pm. He wanted to make good time and realised that to get to his planned destination by 5:00 pm, he would need to go just slightly over the posted speed limit.

It was raining quite heavily as Graham drove through northern France but he was confident that even with the weight of his load, he would still be able to brake and stop properly if he had to make an emergency stop. However, Graham was affected by the glare from the lights of oncoming vehicles. He switched off his headlights and pulled closer to the car in front of him but maintained a two-second gap.

After a long day on the road, Graham finally pulled into the rest area at 6:00 pm. He wanted to get another early start the next day so he took a reduced daily rest period. He hoped to get through customs by 9:00 am and would need to get his papers in order before getting on the road in the morning. As he settled in for the evening and ran through the next day's schedule, he realised that he might have to cross some bridges in the region. He would have to check the truck height in the morning and review the details of his route. Graham had recently seen a photograph in the newspaper showing the damage to a trailer caused by going under a low bridge. He wanted to make sure he did not repeat that truck driver's mistake. The newspaper photo was vivid in his mind and was the last thing he thought about as he drifted off to sleep.

Case Study No.4

Peter was an experienced heavy goods vehicle (HGV) driver. On his next trip, he was to deliver dangerous goods, both nationally and internationally. Peter held the required training certificate and had three years left on his International Carriage of Dangerous Goods by Road (ADR) licence. He also held Certificates of Professional Competence (CPCs) in goods and passenger vehicles and drove both types of vehicle for a living.

Before arriving for work today, Peter completed a reduced weekly rest period. At the depot, he checked out his truck which had two axles and a covered box body. When empty, the truck weighed eight tonnes. Peter performed his walk-around check and cockpit drill.

Peter was asked to drive the pre-loaded truck of packages and containers to a chemical manufacturing plant on an industrial estate about 25 kilometres away. The customer disclosed the dangerous goods and Peter agreed to carry them. He looked at the pre-loaded packages of corrosive chemicals and found that they were labelled correctly. After the delivery, Peter would bring back a tanker loaded with flammable liquid for onward transportation to France. This would be his next job.

Peter's Transport Emergency Card (Tremcard) contained the following information:

- details of the cargo,
- basic personal protection to be used, and
- the immediate action to be taken by the driver if there was a crash.

Peter made sure that his truck complied with the regulations for transporting each type of goods. He also checked that the Kemler plate was displayed and that the international consignment note was in the truck.

Peter arrived safely at his destination and parked in a supervised area. He was given a tanker to take back with him. He checked the new vehicle for roadworthiness and found it to be fine. He also noticed that it only had two axles (a tandem axle). At the weighbridge, the yard supervisor weighed the tanker and gave Peter a receipt. This showed that Peter was up to the weight limit with this truck. Peter was aware that the load was an international consignment.

The tanker had special plates and markings to clearly identify the contents. Peter checked that the correct symbol (based on the classification of the hazardous goods) could be seen on the tanker.

As he drove along the motorway, Peter skipped some of the intermediate gears. It had started to rain slightly. He felt a little drowsy and decided to listen to the radio. As he searched for a good radio station, he did not notice that there was a crash ahead. Suddenly, he heard a loud screech and looked up. Unfortunately, it was too late. Peter slammed on the brakes, lost control, and the tanker rolled over. Flammable liquids began to leak from the tanker.

Witnesses at the crash scene immediately called the fire and rescue services. Peter told them not to use their mobile phones so close to the tanker. The fire and rescue service arrived quickly before the tanker and liquids had a chance to catch fire. Peter told them about the tanker's contents and led the onlookers to safety. Soon a crane arrived to help get the tanker upright. Gardaí diverted traffic and the fire and rescue service cleaned up the spill. Luckily, no one was injured, including Peter.

Peter would not be able to deliver the liquid goods to France. He was worried about the conversation he was going to have with the sender. When he arrived back at his base, he told his boss that he would need a signed and witnessed letter giving details of his rest days during the previous three weeks. He had his digital tachograph card and analogue charts for the last 21 days. Peter finished work, went home, and took a regular weekly rest period. He would contact the sender of the liquid goods in the morning.

Case Study No.5

Larry operated his own haulage business in Ireland and was a regular driver of "low loader" trucks. His job this morning was to collect a new excavator from the Dublin docks and deliver it to a customer in Kerry. When he arrived at work, he changed into his overalls and work boots with protective toe caps. He collected his bag from the locker. This contained Larry's high-visibility wear, work gloves, pencil, pens, clipboard, camera, and first aid kit. Larry then collected his documents and instructions for the journey from the clerk in the office.

Larry checked the address and his road map. In planning his route, he considered the truck's height, weight, and physical restrictions. For this journey, he would be driving a one-year-old truck fitted with the original digital tachograph. After reading his documents, he realised that he would be delivering a heavy, wide excavator to a quarry.

Larry found his vehicle in the depot. He noticed that it was a beaver-tail low loader with four axles. He did his walk-around check and then completed his company's "nil defect" report sheet. He attached this to his clipboard with the other documentation his supervisor had given him. He climbed up into his cab and placed his clipboard inside the glove compartment and asked his helper to get into the truck. He then carried out his cockpit drill. Shortly after moving off, he realised that he had not turned off his mobile phone.

Larry's Cockpit Drill
Gauges working
Documentation
Sufficient fuel
Wheels unchalked
Gear selector
Mirrors
Reflectorised side markings
Map holder

Larry's Walk-Around Check
Brakes
Lights & Indicators
Radio System
Tyres & Nuts/Markers
Horn
Mirrors
Windscreen Wipers & Washers
Vehicle History
Tachograph
Speedometer
Exhaust System
Number Plates

When Larry arrived at the docks he opened the door fully and, facing the cab, climbed down using the steps and grab handles. He then contacted the freight manager, who located the excavator. The manager told him to put on his safety jacket and then load his truck. Larry did as he was asked. The excavator started easily and Larry drove it slowly onto the truck. Once in position, he parked the excavator safely then lowered the machine bucket onto the floor of the truck. He had to use the outriggers on the truck when loading the machine, as the excavator was a little wider than the floor of the truck. Larry then attached restraints onto the lashing points on the truck. Since it was a wide load, he used warning markers fitted with lights, as the day was overcast and it might be dark before he reached his destination. When he was finished, he checked the lights and switched on the amber beacon bar on the cab and a warning beacon on the truck to alert other road users of the wide load. Before leaving the port, Larry completed the consignment note and made sure to keep the correct copy for himself.

Larry's route was along the N7 dual carriageway. While signalling left and slowing to make a tight left turn into St. Margaret's Road, which leads to the N7, Larry noticed a cyclist in his left mirror. The cyclist was beginning to move up the left side (nearside) of the truck. Larry continued to watch his left mirror. He muttered to himself, recalling how the previous day he had encountered a cyclist wearing reflective clothing, riding on the left in the city centre. Larry noticed the cyclist glancing over his right shoulder. Larry heard a horn blow and saw a car approaching on his right side. The car was warning Larry that the rear overhang of the truck had swung into the bicycle's path.

Larry was agitated by these events and, once around the corner, he tried to make up some time. He approached the next right-hand corner a little fast, braking on the corner. He had to steer hard to avoid hitting the kerb.

Once on the dual carriageway the drive went smoothly until the left front of the truck began to shake wildly and the steering wheel began to vibrate. Before Larry could say "blow-out," his tyre burst. Holding the steering wheel firmly, he carefully crossed onto the hard shoulder. A chunk of rubber slapped about inside the wheel arch as Larry brought the truck to a gentle stop. When the lorry was completely stopped, Larry put on his high-visibility vest and told his helper to remain seated while he got off to check the situation. He displayed his warning triangle and tried to stop traffic by waving his arms. When he was unable to stop traffic, he got back into the truck and turned on his hazard warning lights. He then contacted the depot and a repair truck soon arrived to fix the puncture. When the repair had been completed, Larry quickly checked his load.

As he got close to Kerry, he had to slam on his breaks to avoid hitting some sheep that were crossing the road. The excavator rolled towards the cab. Luckily, there were no other vehicles around. He attached extra restraints to secure the excavator. He made it to Kerry within his time window, which was a half-hour short of the industry standard.

Case Study No.6

Robert had a national Road Haulage Operator's Licence and operated within Ireland. He usually carried ceramics, fine glassware, and collectibles, but he also had another truck that he used to carry pigs for local neighbours. Robert was paid cash for carrying his customers' goods.

On today's trip, Robert would be carrying fragile goods. While the packages were being loaded onto pallets and into the truck, Robert checked the quantity, the overall condition of the goods, and the packaging. The fragile goods were packed in appropriate containers labelled "Fragile – Handle with Care". This was a light load and Robert was not sure how to secure it.

The sender and Robert completed a consignment note and the sender kept the correct copy. The customer had chosen Robert to carry the goods because he offered "company's risk" contracts. She also had confidence in road freight and did not want the fragile goods sitting on the railway tracks for a long time.

Once he had secured the load, Robert did his routine walk-around check and cockpit drill to make sure everything was in order.

He set off at 9:15 pm. After driving for four hours, Robert decided to pull into a service area. He parked in the truck parking area and switched off the engine and rested for 45 minutes. Before driving on Robert wanted to make sure the containers were still intact from the journey so far. As he checked the load, he noticed that there were broken strands on some of the ropes. His delivery

Robert's Cockpit Drill
Documentation
Parking Brake
Side Markings
Map Holder
Warning Systems
Gear Selector
Interior Mirrors

Robert's Walk-Around Check
Brakes
Lights & Indicators
Tyres & Nuts/Markers
Horn
Windscreen Wipers & Washers
Tachograph
Speedometer
Exhaust System
Correct Plating
Seat Belts
Reflectors

window was 6:00 am to 8:00 am so he had no time to spare. As his destination was not much further, Robert decided to continue using the same ropes and to discard them after unloading the goods. He arrived at his destination at 8:00 am. When Robert arrived at the Glimmer, Sparkle, and Shine shop, he opened the trailer to check the load and ropes before the customer came out to inspect the goods. He felt guilty about not using new ropes. Fortunately, everything looked as it did when it was loaded the day before. The customer inspected all the boxes and took delivery of the goods. Robert then discarded the frayed ropes.

In preparation for his return journey, Robert checked the truck's tyres, battery, windscreen wipers, mirrors, and brake hoses. He planned his route to avoid traffic congestion. After driving for 15 minutes, he noticed an arch bridge ahead. The headroom under the bridge was 3.9 metres (13 feet) and his truck was 3 metres (10 feet) high so he knew it would fit within the bridge restrictions. As Robert drove under the bridge, he glanced down to change the radio station and, as a result, lightly scraped the left side of the bridge. He did not think there was any damage to the trailer or the bridge. As there were no witnesses, he did not stop or report the incident to the Gardaí.

As he drove, Robert daydreamed about how fortunate he was to be driving road freight and not handling rail freight. Some of his friends who handled rail freight had lost their jobs. Although Robert was regularly away from home for days at a time, he was happy to be a truck driver.

1

2

Case Study No.7

Brenda was aware she had a very long journey from her home town of Buncrana Co. Donegal down to Limerick. She went to the staff canteen and ate a good breakfast, one which would help her concentrate on her driving over the long distance without getting hungry. Brenda's consignment included bricks, bags of cement, and boxes of insulation products. She picked up her keys from the transport manager and, before having her truck loaded, carried out her daily walk-around check and a cockpit drill.

Before helping the fork truck driver to load the truck she set her tachograph to the correct mode. In order to make the loading easier she used a sack barrow to carry the bags of cement. The bricks were distributed throughout the center of the truck. Next, the cement bags were loaded at 90-degree angles. Finally, the insulation boxes were placed around the heavier items. As she had no straps to stop the load from moving, Brenda placed the

Brenda's Walk-Around Check
Windscreen
Wipers
Windscreen
Washers
Legal Discs
Wheel Condition
Tyres
Fuel Filler Cap

Brenda's Cockpit Drill
Doors Secured
Seat Adjustment
Gear Level in
Neutral
Mirrors Set
Fuel Level

tarpaulins on the load, starting from the front and moving towards the back of the truck. She used rope to secure the tarpaulins in place.

Brenda started out early to get to Limerick before lunchtime (where she wanted to take her first break). As usual, she used the National roads as much as possible, watching for traffic signs that indicated things such as danger or speed limits.

Whilst driving through Donegal she encountered numerous uphill and downhill grades, and repeatedly had to change gears. The difficult driving conditions and excessive gear changing caused her to get extremely tired, but in order to make her delivery window in Limerick she kept driving. When leaving Crusheen (a town on her route), she passed under an arch bridge with vehicle restrictions.

At one point along the N 18, she came across a slow moving motorcyclist. She tried to maintain an appropriate speed and distance, but the rider was going much too slowly. If Brenda continued at that speed, her delivery time would be delayed. As the right lane of the dual carriageway was closed for roadwork, she decided to move closer and flash her headlights at the rider, hoping he would pull over into the hard shoulder and let her pass. A Traffic Corps Garda saw what happened and pulled Brenda over to ask her about the incident.

The Garda was aware that some of the drivers who worked for the same company as Brenda had a reputation of tampering with their tachographs. In fact, in a recent news report, he heard that one of these drivers was convicted of "altering with intent to deceive" and received the maximum penalty. The Garda decided to check Brenda's tachograph. He asked her to open the tachograph and remove the chart. He then proceeded to inspect the traces made on it before handing it back to her. The tachograph was all in order, and she had the previous 21 days charts with her. However, he did not ask to see them.

As anticipated, Brenda arrived late to her destination, where she was asked to provide the transport contract documents to the authorised person. The supervisor agreed to unload the truck and, as that gave Brenda an hour and a half, she decided to go off and enjoy her evening meal. She returned at 7:00 pm at which time the staff and the supervisor left, forcing Brenda to finish unloading the last few bags of cement.

At 7:45 pm, when the unloading was complete, Brenda began the return journey which was to take her 6 and a ½ hours. After driving for only 3 kilometers Brenda remembered that she had forgot to change the mode switch on the tachograph to the correct position. She knew that it recorded the speed, distance, and time travelled. Whilst driving and correcting the mode switch setting, she decided to check the chart to make sure it was still recording. Brenda did this by opening the tachograph head whilst driving along the straight stretch of road.

Whilst passing through Oranmore she realized she had not had the consignment note signed. Deciding it was too late to do anything about it now, she kept driving on. Because this had been a long day, she was now feeling very tired. In order to get home as soon as possible she kept driving and arrived back at her depot at 3:30 am.

Case Study No.8

Today, Lorraine was going to drive her three axle, rigid truck fitted with a freezer full of containers of potato scone dough from Dublin to Barcelona. She looked forward to this journey because she had just finished two weeks holiday at home.

Lorraine knew this was an international journey, so she brought her previous tachograph charts for the days she had worked. She was also given a letter of attestation by her employer. She had all the vehicle documentation including the correct operator's licence that she had got four years ago and a European Insurance Accident Report Form. While she was on holiday her truck was serviced, so she did not check her vehicle before using it, since the mechanic should have checked it. She did check the freezer though, because she had been caught before with a faulty freezer, and all of the frozen goods had to be thrown away.

Lorraine's customer was Sorcha's Scones, a well-known distributor of frozen potato scone dough to local markets. Her journey was taking her to Bice's, a small bakery in Barcelona. The loading bay staff took special precautions while loading Lorraine's truck. The potato dough was in containers, stacked on wooden pallets and wrapped in sheeting. Then they strapped the containers to the pallets and secured the pallets to the truck. The loaders parked the truck in the yard and joined it to an electrical connection to keep the freezer at the correct temperature.

After collecting the truck from the yard, Lorraine drove to Dublin Port, boarded the ferry, and used a driver bunk and meal voucher. The ferry arrived in Holyhead. Lorraine knew she had no time to waste in getting to Dover to catch another ferry to Calais. Her truck was one of the first off the ferry. She drove through the customs without delay and onto a clear road. Her journey to Dover began at 10:30 am and took her along the A5 leading to the M6. She had heard from other drivers on the ferry that there were roadworks.

While travelling through the contraflow roadworks on the M6, a traffic patrol car pulled Lorraine over and a police officer asked if she was aware that her rear light cluster was not working properly. When indicating her brake light flashed, and when she used her foot brake one indicator and fog light lit up. The police officer also noticed that the fuel filler cap was missing and the vehicle plate was not attached to the vehicle. Rather, the plate had been stored loosely in the passenger door pocket. So the police officer gave a vehicle probation notice to Lorraine.

Fortunately, the officer allowed her to drive away in the truck, because she was running late for Dover. However, she would not drive over the speed limit, as there were several enforcement cameras on the M25 which had a goods vehicle speed limit of 60 mph (96 km/h).

After driving for ten minutes, a bird dropped down into traffic in front of Lorraine's truck. She braked and swerved to avoid hitting it. The truck almost tipped over, but Lorraine's quick thinking and driving experience kept the truck on all of its tyres. Once back on the roadway, she noticed that the truck was slightly slanted to the right. When she pulled over to the side of the road, she discovered that the right front tyre was flat. She phoned her depot who arranged a company to replace the tyre and with the help of a professional tyre fitter she got back onto the roadway.

Lorraine finally arrived in Dover at 7:15 pm, after driving the 610 km from Holyhead, and caught a ferry to Calais. Once in France, she drove on to Troyes, a journey lasting almost four hours. Following her minimum rest period she drove 1,000 km to Barcelona without stopping. When she arrived at the bakery, she parked the truck and went to her hotel for a well-deserved daily rest period.

The next day at the bakery, it took eight hours to unload the truck because there was no forklift. On the return journey, Lorraine was feeling tired and took a short nap after 800 km. She caught the ferry to Dover and during the crossing she realised she had broken the tachograph rules. She took an old chart and changed the date to suit this journey.

Eventually she got off the ferry and drove down a long steep hill to join the motorway for Holyhead. She had a three-hour delay at Holyhead before the ferry left for Dublin. Once on board the Dublin ferry she replaced the real tachograph disc with the false one. After leaving Dublin port, she met a multi-agency roadside check. An RSA Transport Officer checked her tachograph chart and noticed it had been changed. It was a very stressful day for Lorraine.

1

2

Case Study No.9

Liam was an experienced driver with over 40 years experience working in national and international road haulage carrying various loads and general haulage goods for a Dublin haulage operator. This morning he had to collect a full load of steel girders from a steelyard that was 10 km from his depot in Dublin and take the load to a construction site about 60 km in Arklow.

Liam walked out into the yard to his truck. He was the only driver of the truck, which he checked out as part of the company's defect reporting system. He found everything was okay. After doing his safety checks, he checked the equipment he needed for loading and securing the steel girders:

- a storage box containing chains,
- slings,
- securing clamps,
- lashing clamps,
- webbing straps, and
- nylon rope.

All the equipment was there and the insurance company had inspected, tested, and passed them as serviceable only two weeks ago. He also had a Certificate of Roadworthiness that was two months old.

His truck was fitted with a hydraulic on-board crane and stabilisers rated with a lifting capacity of one tonne. The crane was recently tested and certified, but Liam checked it anyway. He called back into the traffic office and collected his documentation for the journey. The load was the maximum weight he could carry as his truck was 32 tonne GVW (gross vehicle weight).

He arrived at the steelyard, spoke to the yard foreman, put on his steel-toe-capped boots, and moved his truck to where it could be loaded. The yard foreman said the forklift driver would help him in loading. While Liam was chocking his drive axle wheels on both sides of the truck, the forklift driver asked him what he wanted loaded first. Liam calculated the weight of the girders; they were various sizes ranging from 500 kg to 1500 kg. He wanted the load distributed evenly over all axles.

The truck was fitted with road-friendly air suspension. Liam was told that he did not need any special handling equipment to load the girders. He checked that he had put on the vehicle handbrake and he then stayed outside the cab while his trailer was being loaded. While loading the steel girders, one of the 1500 kg girders was damaged when the forklift operator accidentally dropped it. He told Liam about the damage and said that he was not going to load the girder on the truck. Liam agreed not to load the damaged girder.

About 30 km down the road, Liam remembered how difficult the same job was years ago when he had an old Foden truck and trailer with steel spring suspension, crossply tyres, a Fuller 9-speed "crash" gearbox, and all round drum brakes. He was enjoying how much more comfortable his current truck was and was very relaxed listening to a CD. All of the sudden, a car honked steadily at Liam, and he noticed that he had drifted into the right lane and almost hit the other vehicle. He corrected his driving, adjusted his seat, and turned off his CD.

After the incident, Liam was pulled over by Garda and they asked him for his documentation. After he gave the Garda the correct set of documents, the Garda reviewed the documentation and visually checked the truck. When the Garda found no defects, the officer demanded that Liam do a breath test. Once the officer found that there were no offences, he sent Liam on his way without further action.

After arriving at the building site, Liam made sure the ground underneath was stable and strong enough to hold the weight before unloading his truck. He stopped, put on the parking brake, and began unloading the steel. Just before he left, he phoned his boss who asked him to put the truck in the secure compound where it was that morning.

The next day Liam returned to the depot for his next job, which was a truck loaded with cartons of silk cloth. He departed at 9:00 am. He was going to drive 185 km to Galway, then changing trucks and returning with a refrigerated load of salmon caught in the Atlantic Ocean. He was going to bring it about 105 km to Tullamore before driving the remaining 80 km to his Dublin base for a very late lunch break. It would be another long day.

1
2

Case Studies
Buses

Case Study No.1

Before setting off on his day's work, John quickly checked the lights, tyres (including tyre pressures), wipers, and his emergency engine stop. At his first stop he recognised a passenger boarding the bus whom he suspected might be hard of hearing. The previous day she had asked how much the fare would be. John answered, "€1.05," while looking at someone at the back of the bus. The passenger then handed him €5 and took a seat without asking for change. At the time John wondered if she had heard him. This time, when she asked for the fare, he looked her in the eye and said, "€1.05." She smiled and gave him exactly €1.05.

As John pulled into the next stop, he noticed a passenger in a wheelchair and a woman with children. He pulled the bus close to the kerb, stopped, switched off the engine, and left the bus in first gear for safety. He lowered the bus using the kneel facility and also lowered the ramp. The woman and children boarded the bus and sat in the priority seating. John helped the passenger in the wheelchair to the docking area where some passengers were stood; he then lifted one wheel over some debris left by the passengers and applied the wheelchair brake. He drove off smoothly.

The next stop was at the new supermarket which John knew would have more passengers than any of his other stops. The bus was nearly three-quarters full with 35 passengers. John quickly calculated how many more passengers with heavy packages he could take. When he arrived at the supermarket he was relieved to find fewer passengers than he'd anticipated. However, the bus was near capacity, a fact proven by the effort needed to move off.

John pulled away, shifting gears quickly to keep the revs low. His bus was an older model but the company had an excellent maintenance schedule. Also, John usually did small checks of his own such as regularly checking tyre pressures, lights, and the emergency engine stop. After John moved off, he travelled along the road in the opposite direction to the rest of the traffic. However, he approached a right-hand corner too quickly and the passengers were thrown about in their seats. The bus had seatbelts fitted but not all the passengers wore them (the bus was designed as a fully seated bus). John now realised that he hadn't taken a break all day.

Before the next stage of the route, there was a steep hill. Road works had been going on below the hill for about a month. As the bus came down the hill, John took his foot off the accelerator and braked gently. He drove along a dual carriageway (built to motorway standard) at 120 km/h and was stopped by a Garda who asked to see John's documents. The Garda also asked for John's tachograph records. After inspection of the bus the Garda told John that his front near-side tyre was defective. This delayed John and his passengers, forcing him to wait at the roadside to have his tyre replaced.

During the conversation, the Garda also asked, "Did you check the bus before using it today?" John admitted that he had not done a complete check as he was in a hurry and forgot. The Garda then called a vehicle inspector who found more items that John would have found if he had conducted his walk-around check. The vehicle inspector also asked about the vehicle maintenance records and the fault reporting procedure at John's company. The bus was detained until the defects had been fixed. This was embarrassing and expensive for John and the company. John will now be prosecuted for negligence.

1

2

Case Study No.2

Alan had a full load of 70 passengers on board as he started out. His route was along the N-2 dual carriageway. While signalling left and slowing to make a tight left turn into St. Margaret's Road, which leads to the N-2, Alan noticed a cyclist in his left mirror. The cyclist was beginning to move up the left side (nearside) of the bus. Alan continued to watch his left mirror. He muttered to himself, recalling how the previous day he had encountered a cyclist wearing reflective clothing, riding on the left in a contra-flow bus lane. Alan noticed the cyclist glancing over his right shoulder. He usually had nothing against cyclists; in fact, he often went out of his way to double-check his mirrors and give them lots of room. He just wished he could give the careless ones a lesson or two. Alan heard a horn blow and a skid from a motorcycle approaching on his right side. The motorcyclist was warning Alan that the rear overhang of the bus had swung into the motorcycle's path.

Alan was agitated because of these events and, once around the corner, he tried to make up some time. He approached the next right hand corner a little fast, braking on the corner. He had to steer hard to avoid colliding with the kerb. Alan checked his mirror to make sure the passengers on the lower deck had recovered from the sharp turn. He failed, however, to check the passengers on the upper deck.

Once on the carriageway the drive went smoothly until the left front of the bus began to shake wildly and the steering wheel to vibrate. Before Alan could think the words "blow-out" his tyre burst. Taking a firm hold of the steering wheel, he carefully crossed two lanes of traffic to bring the bus to a stop on the right shoulder. A chunk of rubber slapped about inside the wheel arch as Alan brought the bus to a gentle stop. When the bus was completely stopped, Alan put on his high-visibility vest and told the passengers to please remain seated while he got off to check the situation. "Blown tyre for sure," he said while kicking what was left of the rubber. Before getting back on the bus, Alan displayed his warning triangle and tried to stop traffic by waving his arms. When he was unable to stop traffic, he got on the bus and turned on his hazard warning lights.

"We've had a blow-out," he explained to the passengers. "I'll contact my depot. In the meantime, please remain on the bus until another one arrives." No sooner had he contacted the depot than a passenger got up and moved toward the door. "Please, sir, you should remain on the bus. Another one will be here shortly," Alan said.

"I'm just going out for a smoke, if you don't mind," the passenger sniped.

"I'm afraid for safety reasons I'll have to ask you to stay on board, please. If you get off, others will want to do so as well and the traffic is moving at 100 km/h. Someone would surely get hurt," Alan replied.

The passenger stared briefly at Alan, then said, "Alright, I understand what you mean now," before moving back to his seat.

With this incident resolved, Alan quickly checked the passengers, making a mental note of the number of passengers (including children) and those needing special help. He contacted the depot again and reported the total number of passengers, including one in a wheelchair. After what seemed an eternity, a replacement bus pulled up and Alan directed the passengers onto the replacement bus. In the interest of safety and to save time, he loaded all of the luggage onto the replacement bus. He could tell this would be a long day.

1

2

Case Study No.3

Michael has been a PCV driver for many years. He is always professional in his approach to work and conducts vehicle checks (including plates) before taking charge of any vehicle. In his first job as a tour bus driver, Michael noticed that tourists carried a lot of luggage. He learned quickly how to stow and distribute luggage and pay attention to passenger limits. Fortunately, his employer was patient and took the time to explain things like stability, axle weight, the legal limits of each vehicle and the effects of overloading on tyre wear, braking power, and stopping distance.

Michael often travelled on bridges and roads that had a maximum gross weight limit to prevent damage. He knew that the weight difference between an empty bus and a full coach could be as much as 7 tonnes. Michael calculated the gross vehicle weight of his bus using the unladen weight and number of passengers plus an allowance for fuel, passengers, and luggage.

When planning a route, Michael considered the size of the bus. He knew the legal maximum width and length of the buses and coaches he drove as well as the swept area of each bus. In recent years, Michael had observed the introduction of different types of bus lanes. He always liked to get an early start so that he would arrive on time and could use the bus lanes that normally operated between 7:00 am and 7:00 pm. When the road was wet, Michael followed the 4-second rule, a point highlighted in TV road safety campaigns. He was particularly aware of this on motorways where vehicles were travelling at much higher speeds.

Michael's latest assignment involved driving a school bus for a private company for the school year. The bus had an emergency dry chemical fire extinguisher and a warning triangle but no other emergency equipment. It had proper internal lighting and was fully fitted with seatbelts. When necessary, Michael turned on the interior and exterior lights and he used the high intensity fog lights during low visibility.

Michael's bus was fitted with stability control and anti-lock braking (ABS) systems. One morning as he left, he noticed that his ABS light did not go out when the bus started or moved above 5 km/h. All the other lights on the systems warning panel worked normally.

It had begun to rain before Michael started work and it seemed the rain would continue for some time. He had planned his route. However, not far along the road there was a traffic hold-up and Gardai directed traffic onto a diversion route unfamiliar to Michael. On the diversion route, Michael had to deal with low trees, adverse cambers, cables, ESB poles, and some overhead obstructions such as shop blinds hanging over the edge of the road. Michael noticed a road sign giving the gross vehicle weight allowed on this road. Fortunately, this was more than the gross weight of his bus. Eventually, he rejoined his planned route and saw that the cause of the obstruction was a double-deck bus stuck under a railway bridge. The blue lights of the emergency services flashed hypnotically. Michael noticed in his interior mirror that a number of children on his bus were not wearing seatbelts and were standing in the aisle looking out the window.

As he waited for the hold-up to cleared and listened to the sound of the rain, Michael started to feel sleepy. He thought about his years as a PCV driver. During this time, he had seen the scale of private bus and coach services increase. He noticed that a lot of European coach operators were using tri-axle coaches. European Union regulations now governed international transport and the introduction of the euro had done away with currency exchange rate fluctuations. To qualify for international work, Michael would need a European Community licence and a bail bond. His employer would have to comply with international road transport rules.

Finally, the double-deck coach was cleared from the railway bridge and Michael could continue his journey. He looked forward to his next assignment as an international driver.

1

2

Case Study No.4

Sean began his route on a foggy, drizzly morning. He had not got much sleep the night before so he started his shift with a cup of coffee to stay awake and alert. He was in a hurry to start his shift so he rushed through the walk-around check of his vehicle (which was designed to carry standing passengers). He checked the mirrors, glass, brakes, wipers, heating ventilation, gearshift linkage, lights and indicators, tyres, engine oil level, reflectors, doors, and exit. Before starting the engine, Sean also carried out the following checks as part of his cockpit drill: mirrors, handbrake, gears, doors, and seatbelt. He did not think he had forgotten anything.

The figure below shows the items checked by Sean as part of his daily walk-around check and cockpit drill:

Sean's Walk-Around Check
Mirrors
Glass
Brakes
Wipers
Heating ventilation
Gearshift linkage
Lights and indicators
Tyres
Engine oil level
Reflectors
Doors and exits

Sean's Cockpit Drill
Mirrors
Handbrake
Gears
Door seatbelt

As he drove, several oncoming cars repeatedly flashed their headlights at the bus. Suddenly, realising his lights were not on, Sean turned them on full beam. There seemed to be more passengers at the stops this morning and, because of this, Sean worried about a possible time delay due to passengers boarding

At the next stop, Sean saw a passenger in a wheelchair with a large suitcase propped against the chair. He realised there would be a further delay due to picking up this passenger. Sean pulled up close to the kerb and helped the passenger onto the bus. When he bent over to pick up the suitcase, a sharp pain spread across his back. Unable to fully lift the suitcase, he slid it under the seat closest to the door.

Sean then asked the people who were crowded into the designated wheelchair space to move. An older gentleman with a cane refused to move, tapping his leg with his cane as reason to remain. Sean explained that the space was for wheelchairs and was not a designated handicap zone. He asked a group of seated passengers if one of them would please give up his or her seat for the gentleman with the cane. A young man smiled and obliged.

While Sean began fastening the straps that secure the wheelchair frame to the bus, the wheelchair passenger set the wheelchair brakes and also secured one of the straps. Sean double-checked the brakes and the strap the passenger had fastened. As Sean drove away, the young man who had given up his seat stumbled because he had not reached a new seat.

As the day progressed, the fog finally lifted. After Sean entered the motorway, he increased his speed to 70 km/h. His route took him from the motorway to a smaller road through a semi-industrial area. There were now more passengers than seats. Some of the standing passengers had become uncomfortable because the journey had slowed and there were fewer stops. As the bus travelled on, an articulated lorry sped around the bus, obviously too fast for the road. The lorry then turned left at a blind corner. Sean's route took the bus around the same blind turn. Once around the corner, Sean saw that the trailer had hit the bottom of a railroad bridge. To avoid delay, Sean quickly turned left onto an adjacent street, causing some standing passengers to fall into each other. Several passengers pointed out that this street was not on the route but Sean replied that he would still make their stops as he knew how to quickly get back onto the route. He decided to report the articulated lorry accident when he got back to the station as he was already running late.

One of the passengers became irate and demanded to get off the bus. Sean looked for a safe place to pull in. He saw yellow lines but there were no "No Parking" signs along the street so he pulled in and stopped. After the passenger got off, Sean turned off the engine and got out of the bus to do a quick inspection of the bus's exterior. Everything looked fine so he continued the journey.

Case Study No.5

Ciara drove a fully seated coach (with no standing capacity) between major cities. This was a kneeling-type coach, equipped with a hydraulic system which allowed the step level to be raised and lowered. Ciara was familiar with the system, its safe operation and secure storage of the equipment.

The picture below shows a ramp.

The picture below shows a lift.

Several elderly and special needs passengers depended on the coach service for mobility. If asked, Ciara helped these passengers. One passenger who was visually impaired often took the coach to visit friends in another city. This passenger needed help in finding an available seat. Ciara always used the kneeling facility for passengers who she thought it helped without being asked.

The picture below shows the type of cane that visually impaired people sometimes use as a mobility aid.

When Ciara picked up her visually impaired passenger this morning, she helped her to find a seat, stowed her luggage, and assumed that her destination was the same as usual.

Today was more eventful than most. At the beginning of the trip, Ciara discovered that there was an extra passenger on the bus. After a quick check, she found the unauthorised passenger and he got off the bus without incident.

During a brief comfort break (a toilet break), Ciara noticed someone in a hooded jacket open the luggage compartment of the bus and dig through the luggage. Luckily, a Garda was nearby. Ciara called the Garda over and she and the Garda approached the suspicious person who quickly turned around, obviously startled. He explained that he was a student looking for his book bag. Ciara quickly unloaded the luggage, stacking it in a pile to her side, until the book bag was visible. The Garda began to bring the student and his bag inside the building for questioning but Ciara indicated that it was probably an innocent mistake. She had seen the student's ID and had spoken briefly with him during the trip. The Garda insisted upon questioning the passenger.

When loading the luggage into the under-floor luggage lockers, Ciara placed the larger, heavier luggage in first. She remembered the unattended bag she had found on another trip earlier in the week. During a stop, she had brought this bag into the station and when no one claimed it, she left it with the ticketing agent.

Once back on the motorway, Ciara noticed that she was travelling at 90 km/h and changed her speed to match the speed limit. Since the luggage and passenger load were lighter than normal, she could tell the difference in the bus handling and found the accelerator and brakes to be more responsive than usual, especially when she was slowing or accelerating. On occasion, cross winds on exposed areas of the motorway rocked the coach. When leaving the motorway slip road, which turned sharply to the left on approach to the roundabout, luggage fell from the overhead luggage compartments. The previous week, when Ciara was driving a full bus around a sudden corner, some of the bags fell from the overhead compartment. Some passengers complained about the falling bags and said they had been jostled. Several passengers made a formal complaint about this incident.

Case Study No.6

Ashling was not familiar with the bus she drove today. She wondered how to find the information she needed about the dimensions, weights, seating capacity, maximum speed, and overhangs of the bus. She expected to have a full bus and so it would be particularly important to know the gross vehicle weight. Ashling was not sure how to calculate the gross vehicle weight. She had already checked the bus before she set out, checking the contents of the first aid kit and its location, the gauge on the fire extinguisher, the emergency hammers, and that the emergency exits were unlocked.

Ashling began her morning route thinking about the safety and comfort of the passengers. Her route contained several hills and she usually had a full bus.

Ashling had difficulty driving safely while trying to keep to her schedule. On downhill slopes, she tended to have trouble with braking. Sometimes the brakes overheated. Ashling was not sure how to use the hand-operated retarder correctly. As a result, she overused the foot brake. In addition, she failed to correctly use the "holding gears" (1, 2, 3 and so on) in the automatic gearbox fitted to her bus. She also took the corners too fast, causing passengers to complain.

The diagrams below show how forces in a moving vehicle affect passengers.

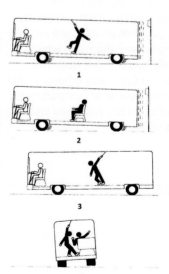

1

2

3

4

While turning left into a side road, Ashling correctly adopted a wider position farther out in her lane.

Driving along the new road, just past an arch bridge with a restriction sign, Ashling saw an older woman with a large piece of luggage. She stopped the bus for the passenger to board with her luggage. Ashling signalled and quickly moved off while the passenger was finding a seat. She heard a horn sound as she pulled away and noticed a motorcycle overtaking her. Ashling did not notice that the luggage was not stored. She was forced to brake hard, throwing the luggage along the aisle and injuring a passenger. Ashling made a right-hand turn into Barrow Street, a street with bollards at the entrance.

As Ashling built up speed, one of the passengers told her that smoke was coming from the rear of the bus. Ashling stopped the bus and opened the front door, which she remembered her instructor saying was the primary emergency exit. She told the passengers to get off the bus and directed them to a safe place. She then called the fire brigade. In pushing toward the door, some of the passengers fell. When the last passenger got off the bus, Ashling checked to make sure that all passengers were indeed off. She grabbed the fire extinguisher (required on all buses) and ran outside to find the source of the smoke. She knew that the smoke source would have to be found and corrected before the bus could continue its journey. She discovered that the smoke was coming from a tyre on the nearside rear axle.

The diagrams below show the bus's dimensions.

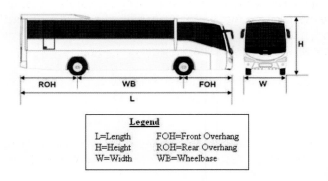